FolderGames
for Phonics Plus

by Lillian Lieberman
illustrated by Marilynn G. Barr

Publisher: Roberta Suid
Copy Editor: Carol Whiteley
Production: Marilynn G. Barr

Entire contents © 1995 by Monday Morning Books, Inc.

For a complete catalog, please write to the address below:
P.O. Box 1680, Palo Alto, CA 94302

Monday Morning is a registered trademark of
Monday Morning Books, Inc.

ISBN 1-878279-85-8

Printed in the United States of America

987654321

TABLE OF CONTENTS

Introduction

FolderGames for Phonics Plus presents activities to enrich reading skills for first through third graders in easy-to-make-and-use file folder set-ups. The folders can be used with individual children, small cooperative groups, or in learning centers.

The activities in *Phonics Plus* help to reinforce skills in decoding, comprehension, word structure, and spelling in an enjoyable format. The activities that focus on decoding range from sound-symbol associations of blends, digraphs, and trigraphs to vowel phonograms. Children are engaged in such work as matching paw print blends with words in bear tracks, racing across a consonant digraph bridge, and finding the r-control words in a lion's dinner. The learning fun also covers following directions, using high-level inferencing, understanding cause and effect, and recognizing the main idea. A variety of hands-on responses, including placing objects, clipping on clothespins, and turning a spinner, keep the children actively engaged.

Each *FolderGames* activity includes the file folder layout and the activity to be duplicated, simple directions for use, and a suggested book to read. This book may be used to help initiate the activities and to enhance the children's enjoyment and involvement in learning. A tab label and an illustration for the folder cover are also provided. Place the directions below the cover illustration to facilitate use. General construction and use directions follow here. The "How to Make Instant Folders" section provides additional information for particular activities.

General Directions

Construction

Use sturdy colored file folders for the instant folders. Duplicate the inside file folder set-up, the illustration for the activity, and the activity label. Color with felt pens, colored pencils, or crayons. Then trim and cut out. Glue the file folder set-up to the inside of the folder and the illustration to the outside front. Glue the directions with the "Book to Read" reference below the illustration. Glue the tab label onto the file folder tab. Laminate both sides of the file folder.

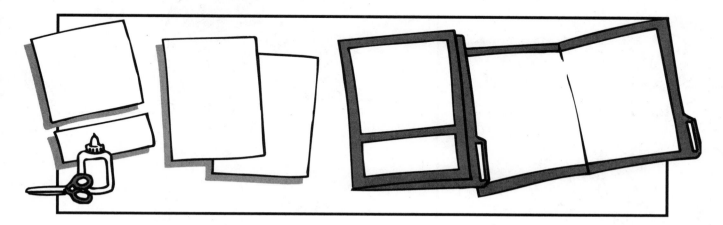

Glue the activity cards, along with any loose parts, such as markers or spinners, onto oak tag for sturdiness. Color and laminate. Cut out or trim as necessary and complete construction. A craft knife is recommended for making the slits and slots for the activities that require them. Buttons or other objects can be used for markers that are not provided. Keep all loose activity parts in a 7 1/2" x 10 1/2" manila envelope with a clasp glued to the back of the file folder.

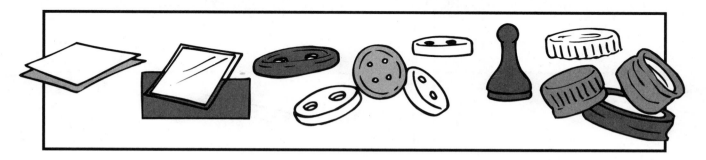

Activity Use

Have the children take out any loose parts from the envelope and open the file folder on the work area. Instruct the children on how to play, referring to the directions. Have the children replace the parts in the envelope after play and deposit the folder in a file basket.

How to Make Instant Folders

Match-ups and Game Boards
(Activities 1-5 and 10-13)

Follow the general directions. For "Wild Card Cricket Race," provide a die.

Clothespin Matches
(Activities 15-21, 28-29, and 33-34)

Follow the general directions. Cut out and glue the labels securely to clothespins. Reinforce with clear sealing tape if desired. Cut out the parts for the file folder set-up. Laminate and glue to the file folder. Leave free of glue the areas where clothespins will be attached. Cut out the extra activity. Color and laminate. Place in the manila envelope. For "Sandwich It!," "Witch's Brew," and "Seal Pups," provide four to six blank clothespins to use with the activity cards. For "Lizards' Tails" and "Cycle Away!," enclose a washable felt pen or erasable crayon and a soft tissue or rag in the envelope.

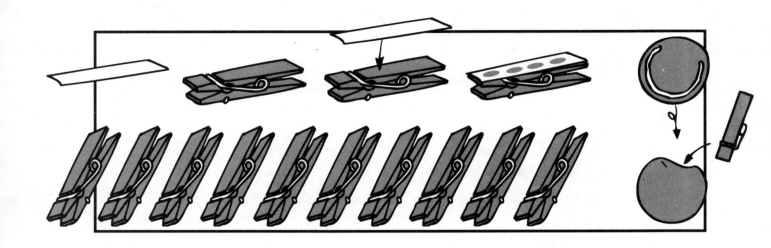

Slip-ins
(Activities 22-23)

Follow the general directions. Glue the loose parts to oak tag. Color, laminate, and place in a manila envelope. For "Eager Beavers," use a craft knife to make slits in the logs on the dotted lines. Spread glue on the outer edges of the beaver dam set-up but leave the area around the slits free of glue. Do the same for "Treasure Boxes."

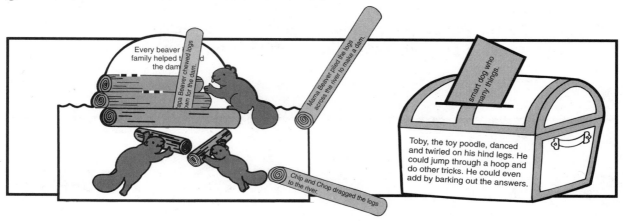

Write-ins and Draw-ins
(Activities 14 and 24-27)

Follow the general directions. Laminate the folder and extra activity cards for a washable or wipable surface. Enclose in an envelope the extra activity cards, a washable pen or erasable crayon, and a soft tissue or rag.

Spinner Set-ups
(Activities 6-9 and 30-32)

Follow the general directions. Duplicate parts for the spinners and wheels and any loose set-up parts. Color and glue to oak tag. Laminate and cut out. Punch a hole in the center of the wheel and attach the spinner with a brass fastener. Place the wheel and the markers in the manila envelope. For "Lion's Dinner!," place meat shapes with the spinner in the envelope. For "Squirrel at the Wheel," "Goosey Goosey Gander," and "Hamster's Wheel," attach the wheels to the folder. Enclose activity cards with a washable felt pen or an erasable crayon in an envelope with a soft tissue or rag.

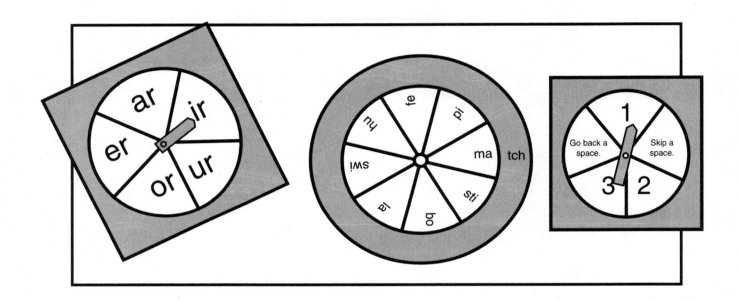

1

Cookie Jars

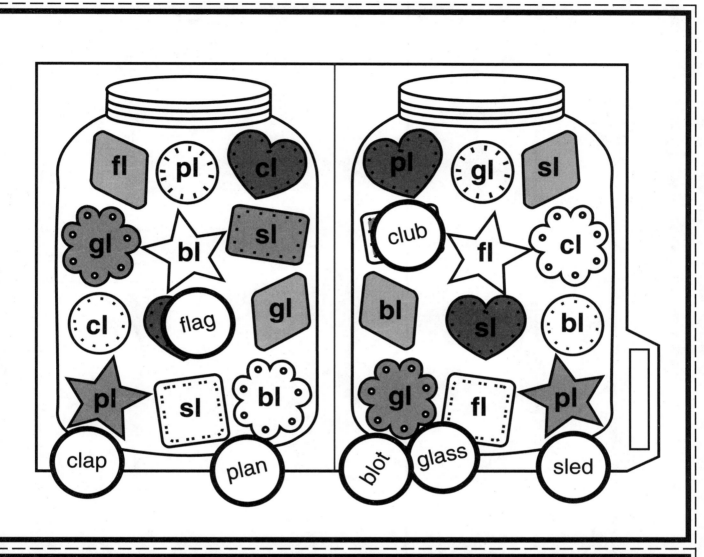

Cookie Jars

Initial consonant blends: fl, cl, pl, bl, gl, sl

Directions: Two children may play. Take out the word cards and place them face down. Open the folder and choose a cookie jar. Take turns turning a card over. Read the word. If the word matches a consonant pattern on a cookie in your cookie jar, put it on the cookie. If there is no match, put the card back on the playing area. See who fills his or her cookie jar first.

A book to read: If You Give a Mouse a Cookie by Laura J. Numeroff

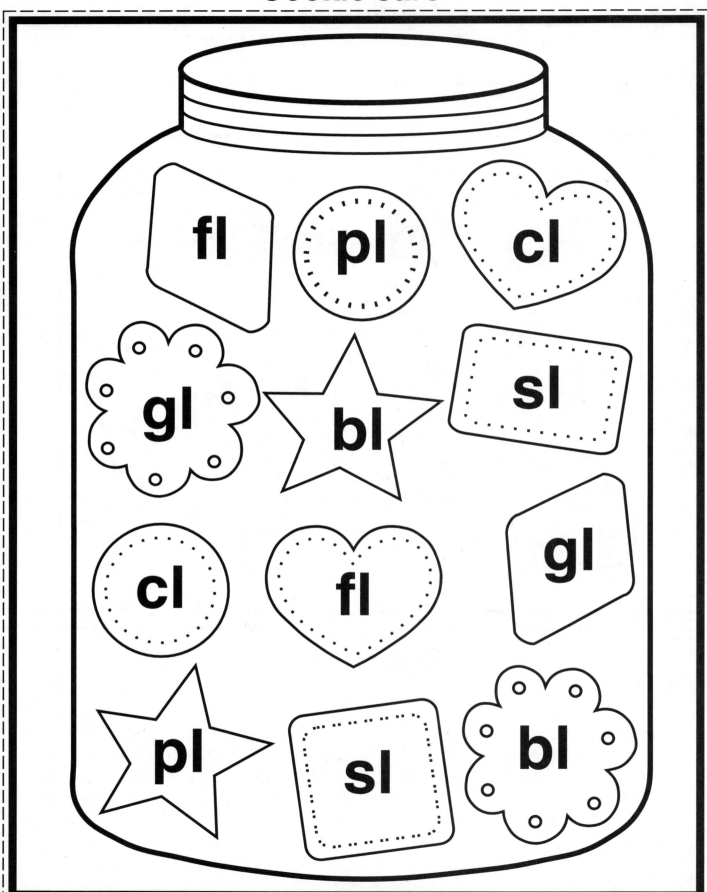

Cookie Jars

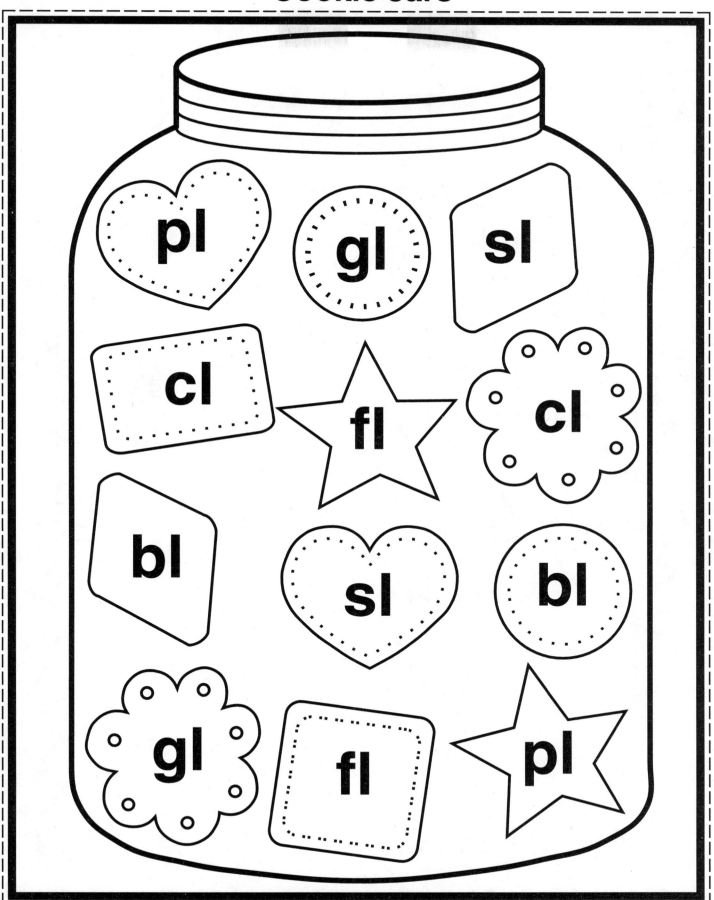

Cookie Jars

flip   flag   fluff   fled

clap   club   cliff   cloth

plug   plan   plot   plush

blob   bless   bluff   blot

glib   glum   glass   glob

sled   slam   slot   slid

2

Bear Tracks

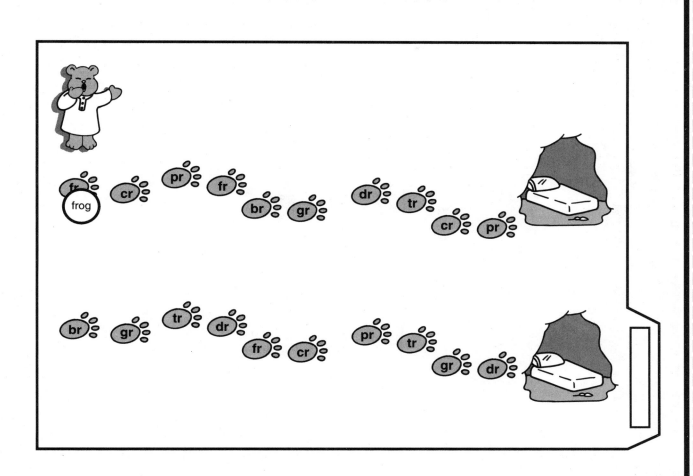

Bear Tracks

Initial consonant blends: fr, cr, pr, br, gr, dr, tr

Directions: Two children may play. Take out the word cards and the two sleepy bears. Place the word cards face down on the playing area. Open the folder and choose a bear track trail. Take turns turning a word card over. Read the word. If the word matches the consonant pattern on your first bear paw print, put the card on it. Put the card back if it doesn't match. The first player to get to the bear den can put a sleepy bear to bed!

A book to read: <u>Animal Tracks</u> by Arthur Dorros

Bear Tracks

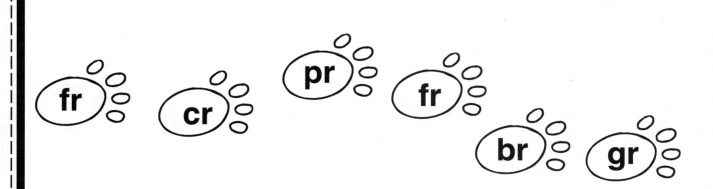

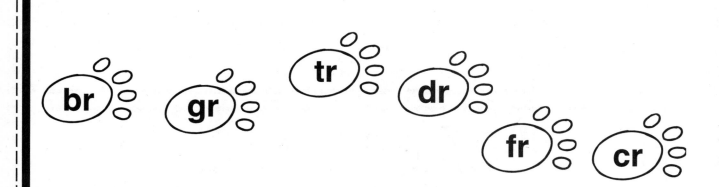

Bear Tracks

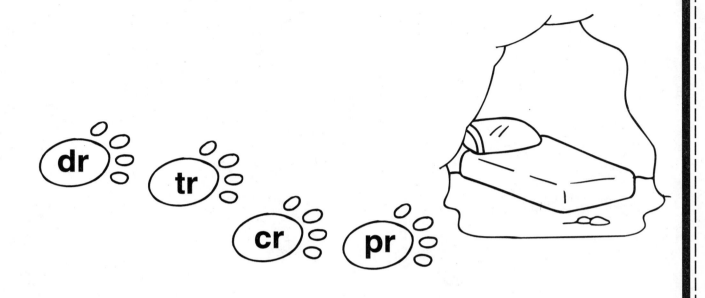

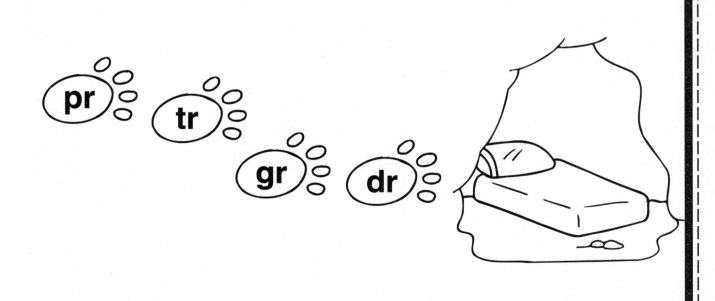

Bear Tracks

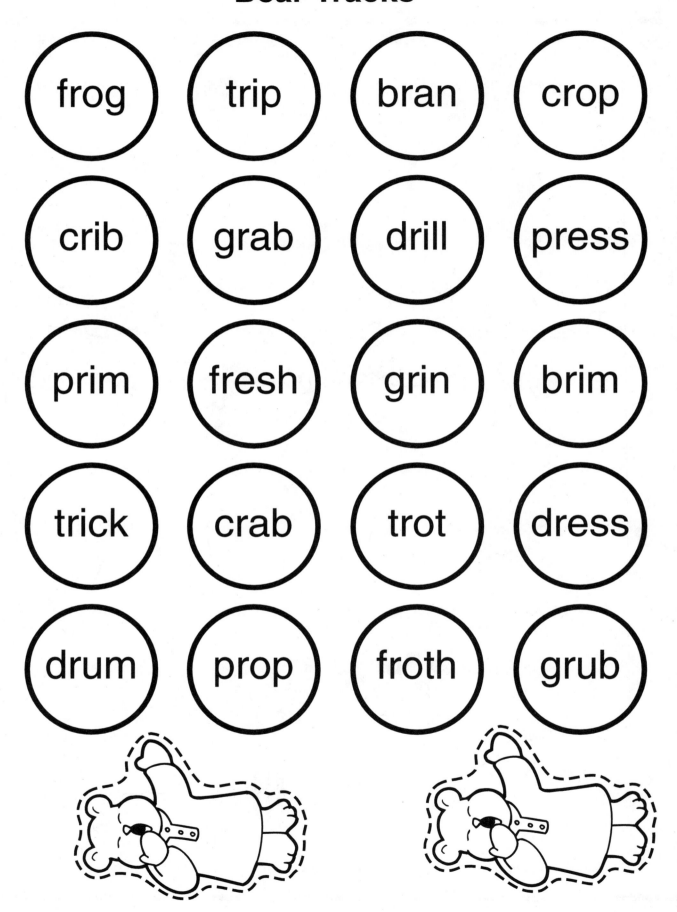

frog trip bran crop

crib grab drill press

prim fresh grin brim

trick crab trot dress

drum prop froth grub

Spider Webs

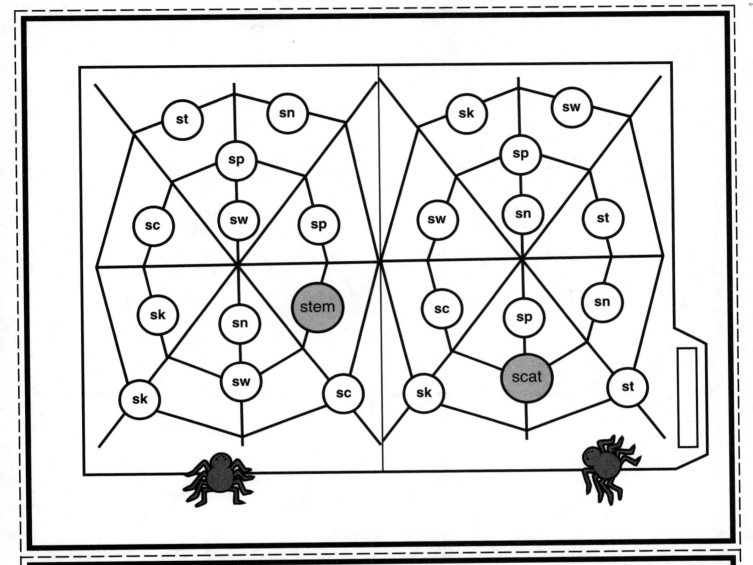

Spider Webs

Initial consonant blends: st, sn, sp, sc, sw, sk

Directions: Two children may play. Take out the word cards and the two spiders. Place the word cards face down. Open the folder and choose a spider web. Take turns turning a word card over. Read the word. If the word matches a consonant pattern on your web, put the card on it. The first player to match all the blends can put a spider on the web.

A book to read: The Very Busy Spider by Eric Carle

Spider Webs

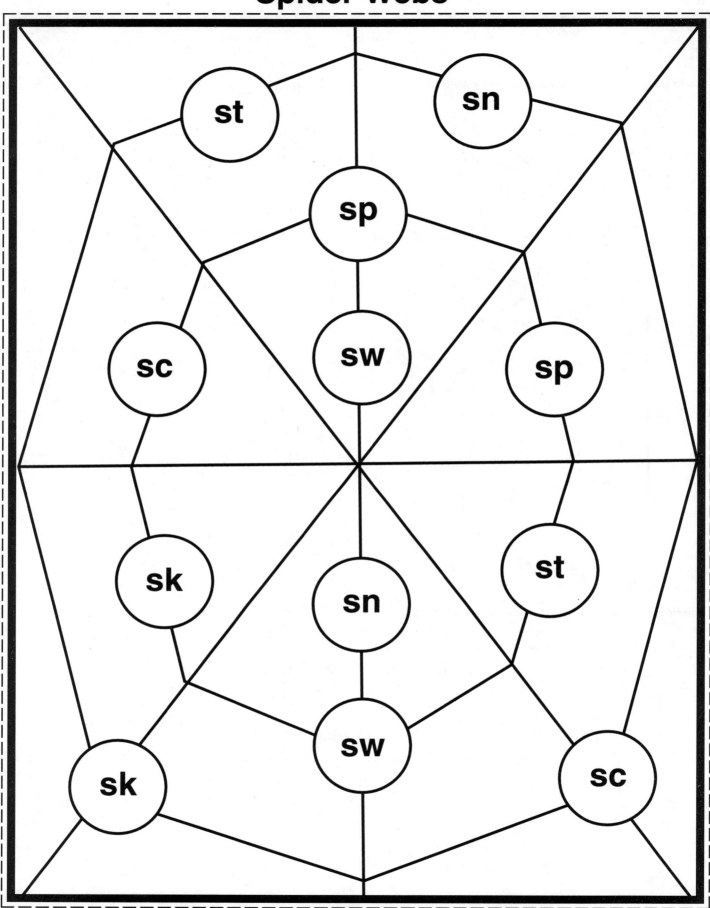

18

Spider Webs

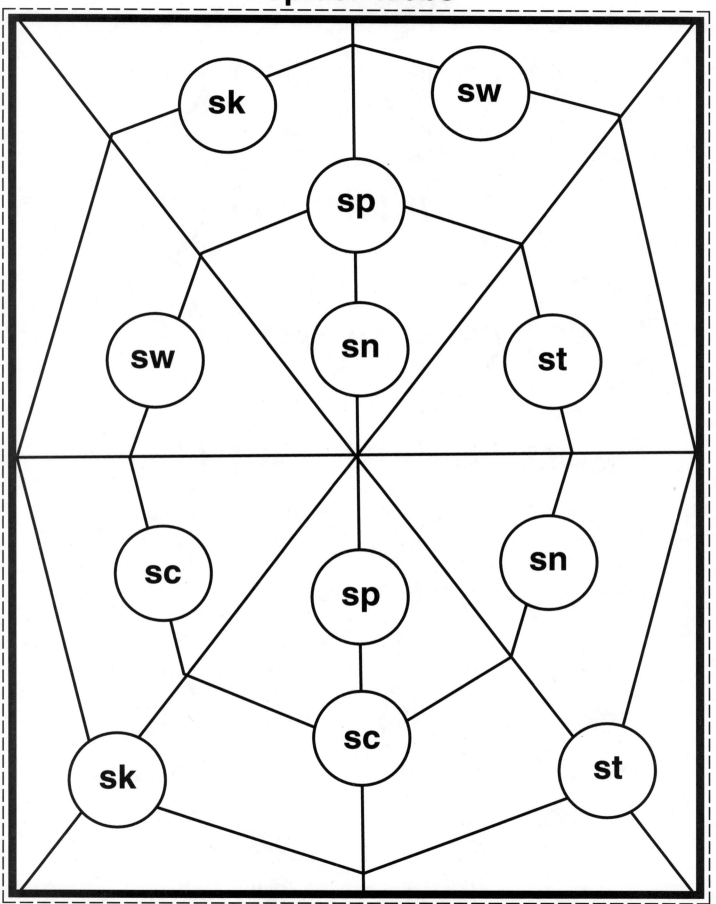

19

Spider Webs

stem stop stiff step

snip sniff snag snug

span spell spot sped

scuff scan scat scoff

swim swift swell swig

skill skunk skull skin

20

Turtles in the Sand

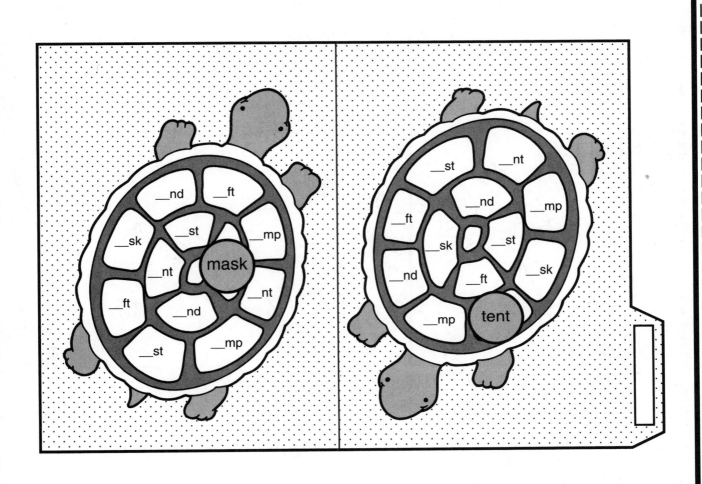

Turtles in the Sand

Final consonant blends: nd, nt, ft, st, sk, mp

Directions: Two children may play. Take out the word cards. Place them face down. Open the folder and choose a turtle. Take turns turning a word card over. Read the word. If the word matches an end consonant pattern on the turtle, put it on it. See who can fill all the spots on his or her turtle first.

A book to read: The Smallest Turtle by Lynley Dodd

Turtles in the Sand

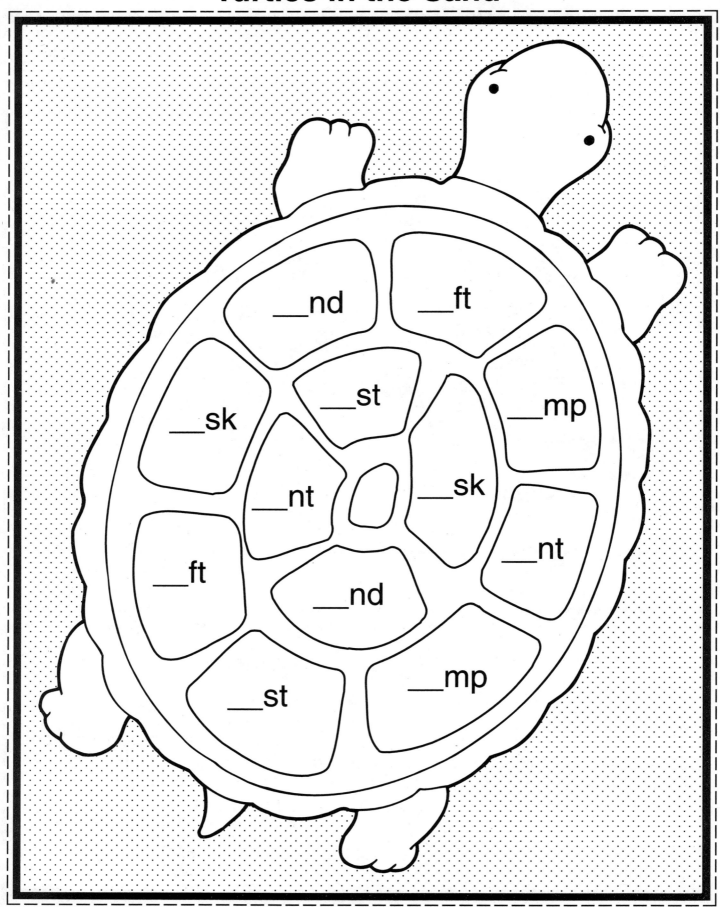

Turtles in the Sand

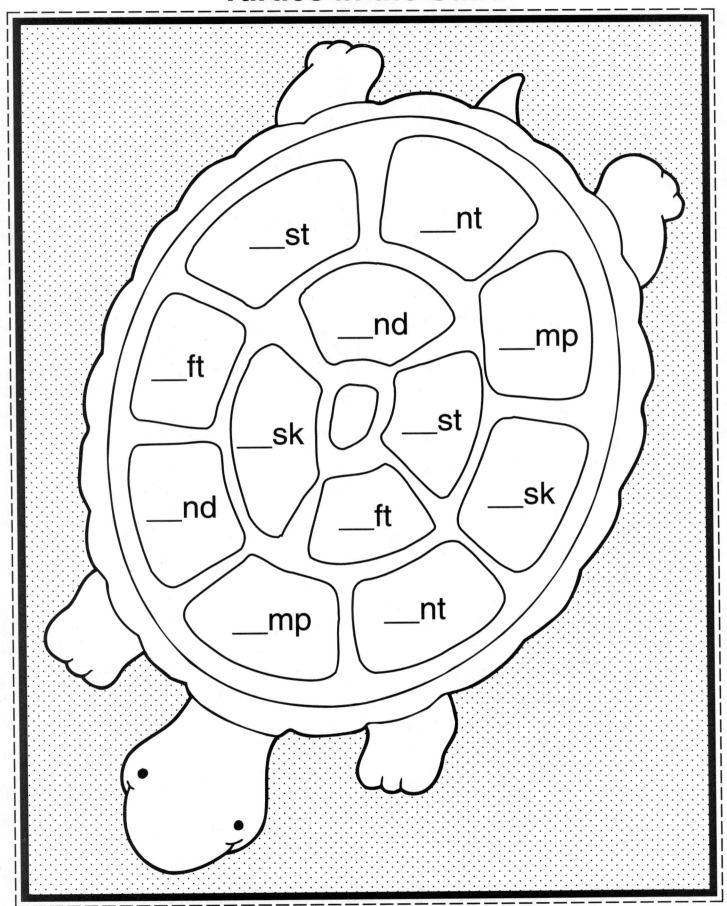

23

Turtles in the Sand

bend   pond   send   land

tent   bunt   vent   pant

raft   left   soft   sift

list   past   dust   pest

mask   husk   risk   tusk

camp   limp   lump   ramp

5

Shoe Shop

Shoe Shop

Initial consonant digraphs: ch, sh, th, wh

Directions: Two children may play. Take out the word cards and place them face down. Open the folder and choose a side. Take turns turning a card over. Read the word. If the word matches a consonant pattern on a shoe, put it on the shoe. See who can find all the shoe matches first.

A book to read: Big Shoe, Little Shoe by Denys Cazet

Shoe Shop

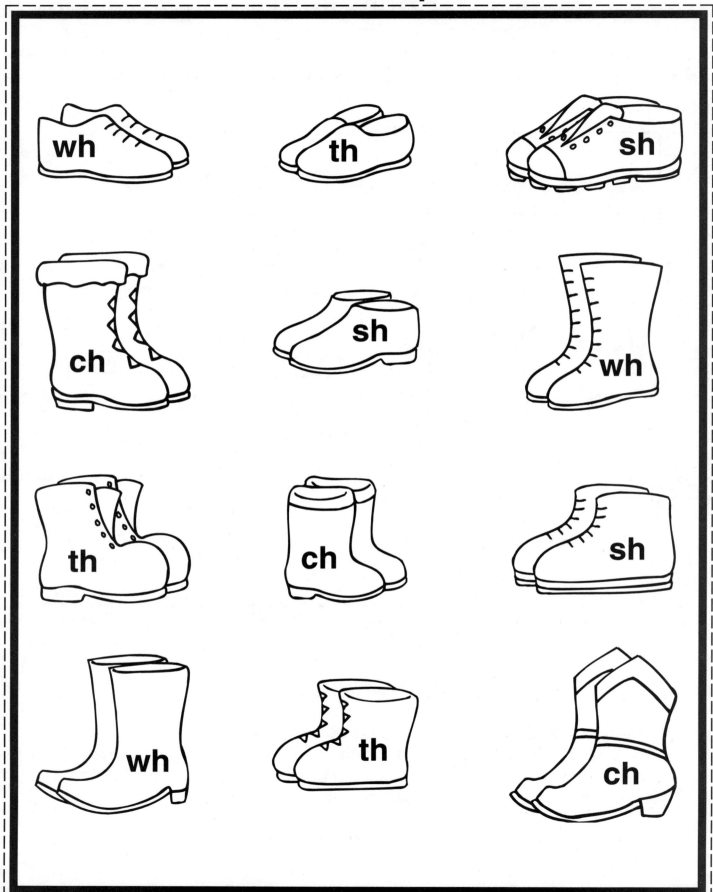

Shoe Shop

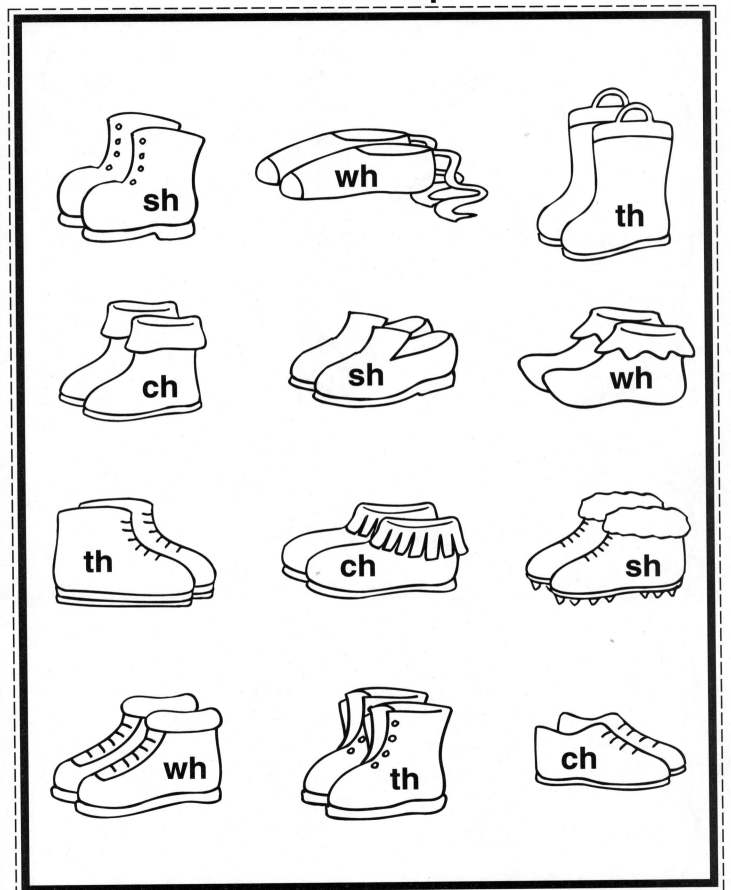

27

Shoe Shop

chin	ship	whip	then
chip	shop	whiff	this
chug	shed	when	that
chap	shell	whim	them
chop	shag	whop	thus
chill	shod	wham	the

6

Trolls on the Bridge

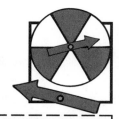

Trolls on the Bridge

Final consonant digraphs/trigraphs: ck, sh, th, tch, dge

Directions: Two children may play. Take out the spinner and the troll markers. Open the folder and choose a bridge. Take a troll. Spin the spinner in turn. If the spinner points to a number, go that many spaces on your bridge. If it points to a direction, follow the direction. Read the word you land on and put your troll on the space. See which troll gets across the bridge first.

A book to read: Trouble with Trolls by Jan Brett

Trolls on the Bridge

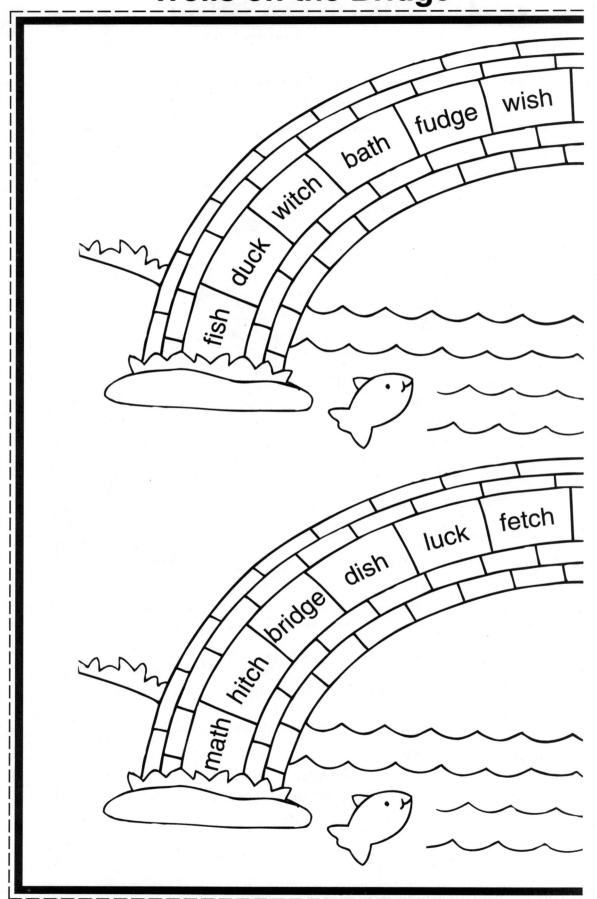

Trolls on the Bridge

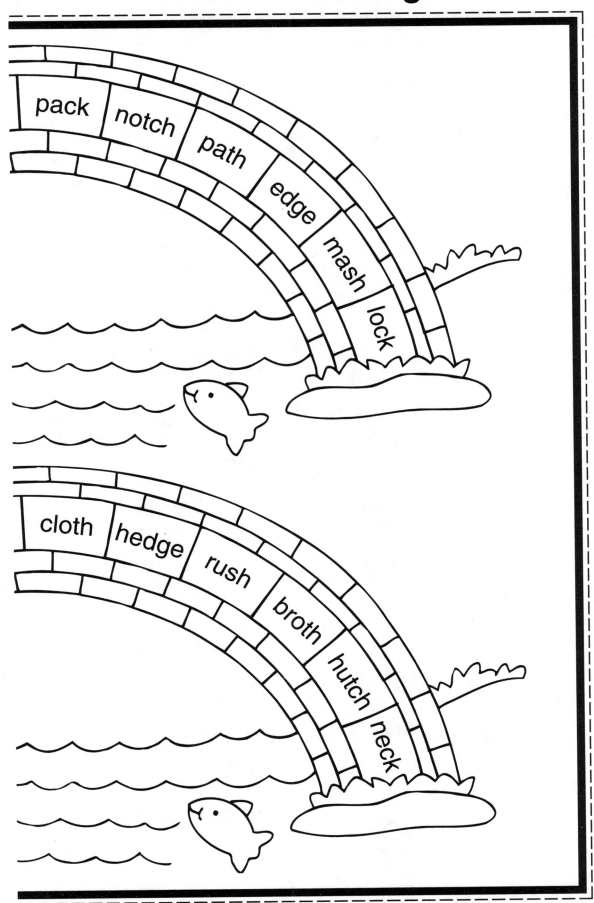

pack   notch   path   edge   mash   lock

cloth   hedge   rush   broth   hutch   neck

31

Trolls on the Bridge

7

Bees to the Hive

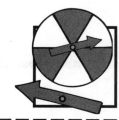

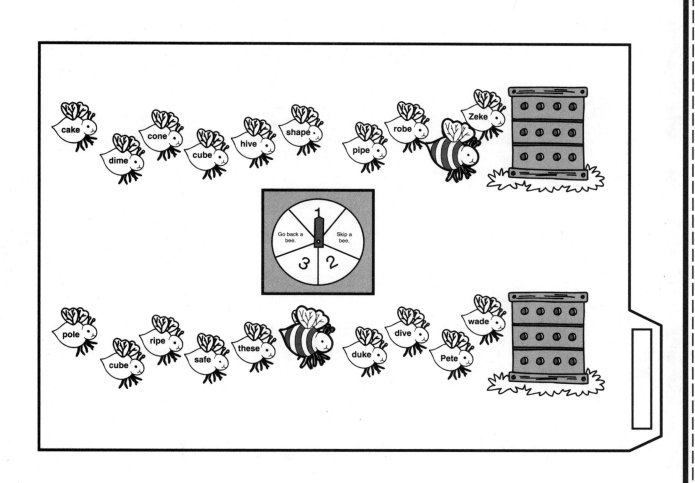

Bees to the Hive

Final e words: a-e, i-e, o-e, u-e, e-e

Directions: Two children may play. Take out the spinner and the two bee markers. Open the folder and choose a bee line. Take a bee marker. Spin the spinner in turn. If the spinner points to a number, go that many bee spaces. If it points to a direction, follow the direction. Read the word you land on and put your bee on the bee space. See whose bee gets to the hive first.

A book to read: <u>All Kinds of Bees</u> by Dorothy E. Shuttlesworth

Bees to the Hive

34

Bees to the Hive

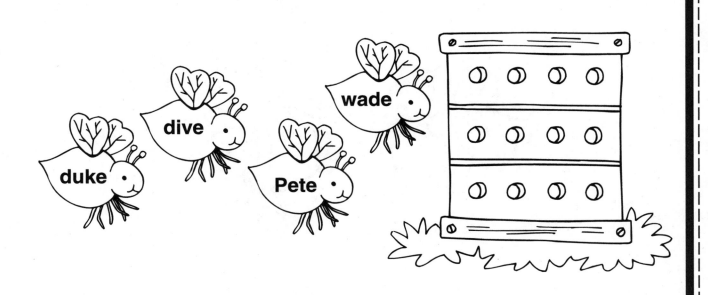

35

Bees to the Hive

8

Lion's Dinner!

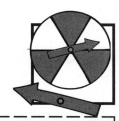

Lion's Dinner!

R-control: er, ir, ur, or, ar

Directions: Two children may play. Take out the spinner and the meat shapes. Open the folder and choose a lion. Spin the spinner in turn. Check the r-control that the spinner points to. Match it with a word on the lion's plate that has the same r-control. Read the word and put a piece of meat on it. See who can fill his or her lion's plate first.

A book to read: The Happy Lion by Louise Fatio

Lion's Dinner!

spur torn dark

bird fern

born charm

surf turf

perch skirt cork

Lion's Dinner!

Lion's Dinner!

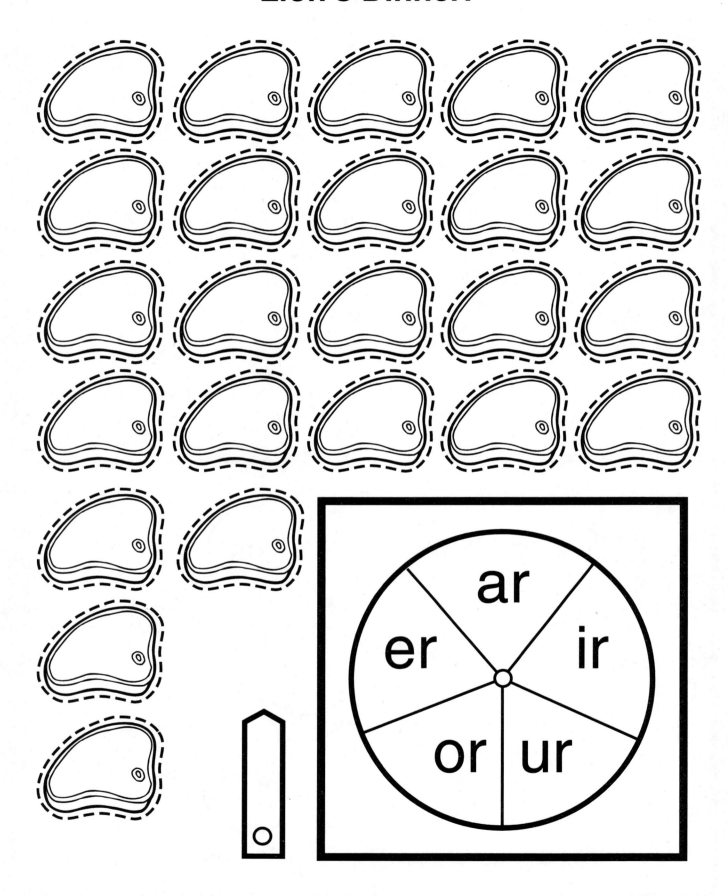

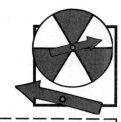

9

Toad Race

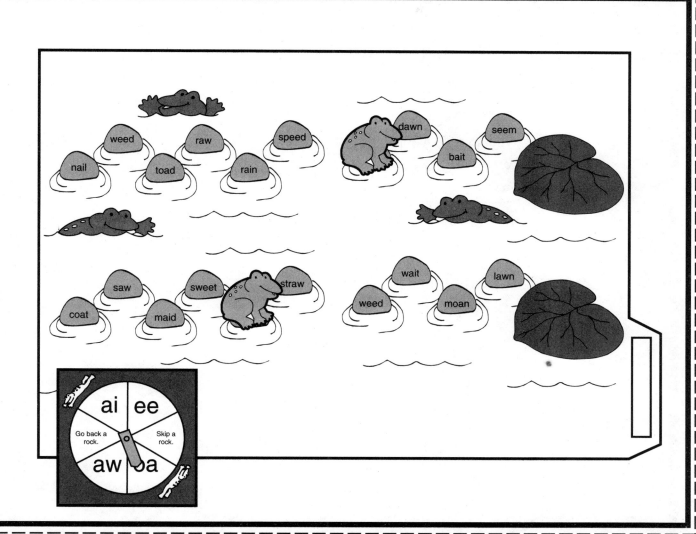

Toad Race

Vowel phonograms: ai, oa, ee, aw

Directions: Two children may play. Take out the spinner and the two toads. Open the folder and choose a rock pathway to the lily pad. Take a toad. Spin the spinner in turn. If the spinner points to a vowel pattern that matches the word on your first rock, read the word and put your toad on it. If there is no match, wait for your next turn. See whose toad gets to the lily pad first.

A book to read: <u>Frog and Toad Together</u> by Arnold Lobel

Toad Race

Toad Race

dawn

seem

load

bait

wait

lawn

weed

moan

Toad Race

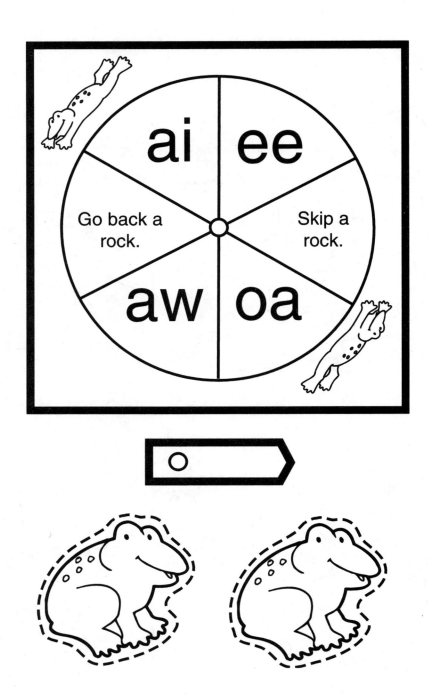

10

Brown Cow

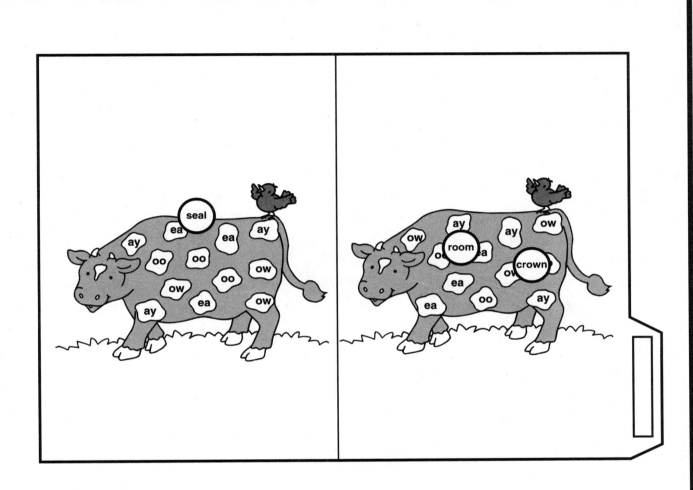

Brown Cow

Vowel phonograms: ay, ea, ow, oo

Directions: Two children may play. Take out the word cards and place them face down. Open the folder and choose a cow. Take turns turning a word card over. Read the word. If the word matches a vowel pattern spot on your cow, put the card on it. See who can fill his or her cow's spots first.

A book to read: Moo, Moo Brown Cow by Jakki Wood

Brown Cow

Brown Cow

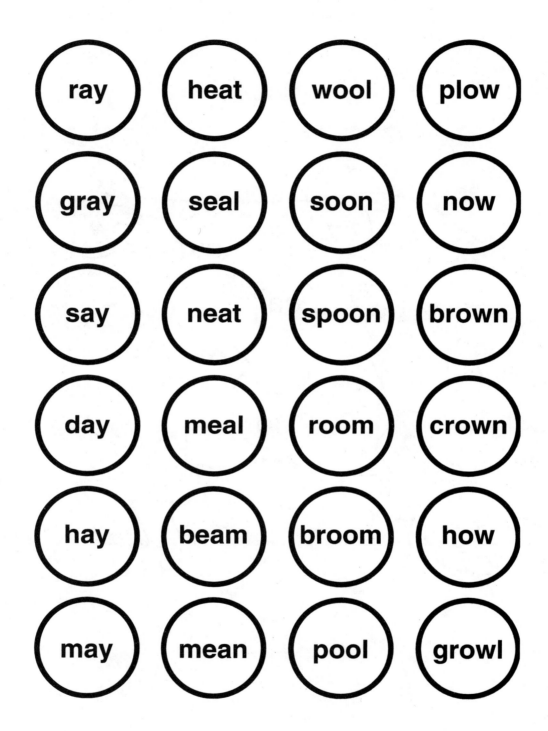

ray   heat   wool   plow

gray   seal   soon   now

say   neat   spoon   brown

day   meal   room   crown

hay   beam   broom   how

may   mean   pool   growl

11

Crow's Nest

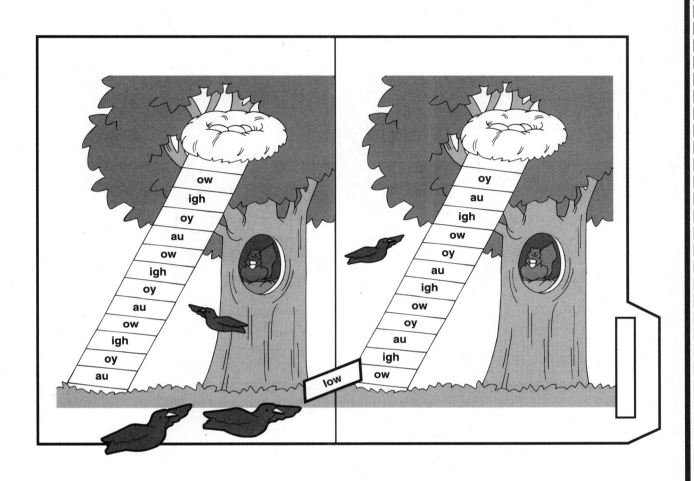

Crow's Nest

Vowel phonograms: ow, igh, oy, au

Directions: Two children may play. Take out the word cards and the two crows. Place the cards face down. Open the folder and choose a tree ladder. Take turns turning a word card over. Read the word. If the word matches the first vowel pattern at the bottom of the tree ladder, put it on the space. If it doesn't match, put the card back and wait for your next turn. The player who gets all the way up the ladder first can put a crow in the nest.

A book to read: <u>No, No Sammy Crow</u> by Lillian Hoban

ow

igh

oy

au

ow

igh

oy

au

ow

igh

oy

au

Crow's Nest

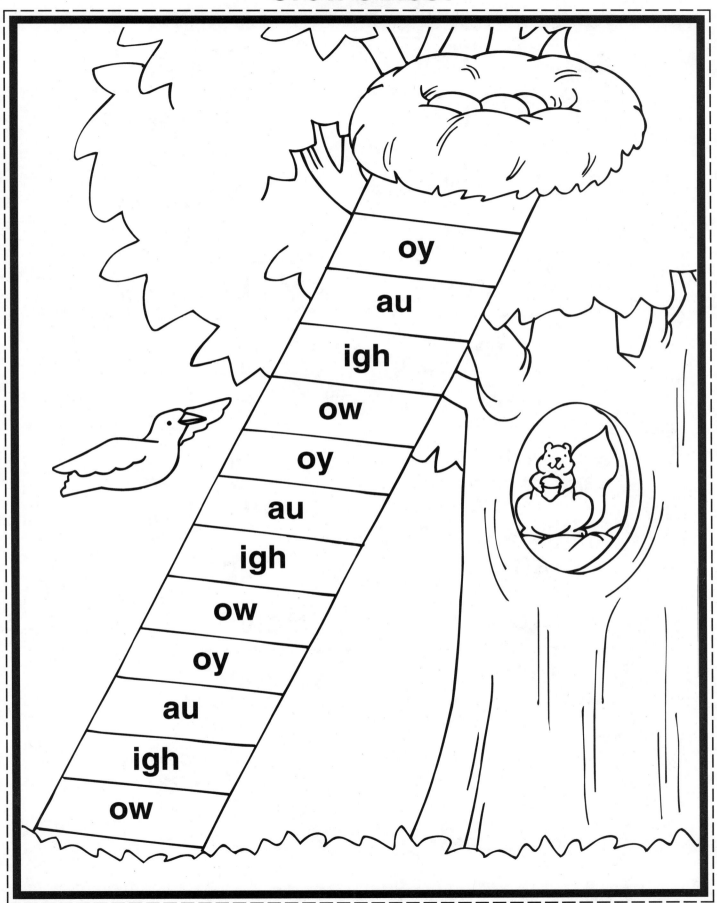

oy

au

igh

ow

oy

au

igh

ow

oy

au

igh

ow

Crow's Nest

coy	sight
joy	light
Roy	tight
boy	high
ploy	bright
toy	flight
row	haul
mow	haunt
grow	launch
slow	jaunt
crow	taunt
low	haunch

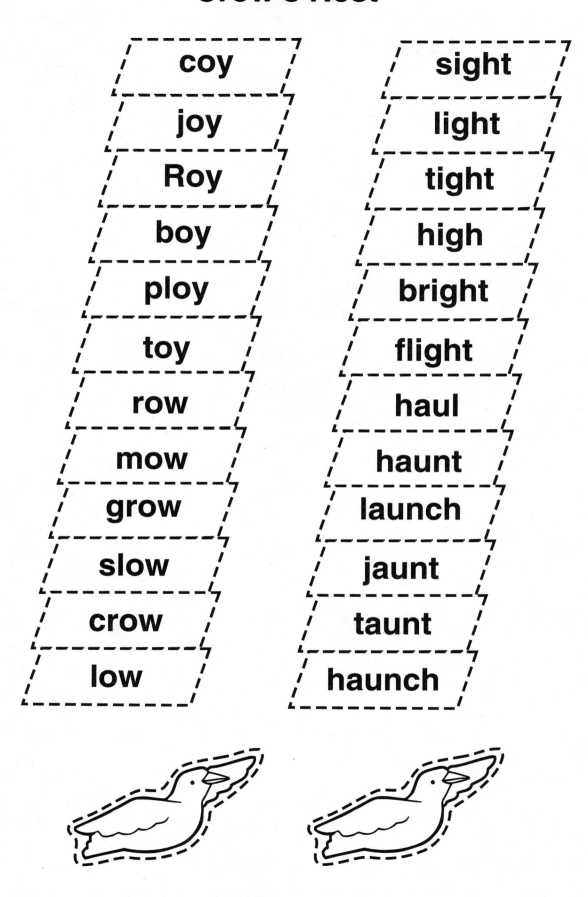

12

Freight Train

Freight Train

Vowel phonograms: oi, eigh, ew, ou

Directions: Two children may play. Take out the word train cars and the two engines. Place the word cards face down. Open the folder and choose a railroad track. Take turns turning a word card over. Read the word. If your word matches the first vowel phonogram on the track, put it on the space. If it doesn't match, put the card back and wait for your next turn. The first player who gets to the end of the track can put the engine at the head of the cars.

A book to read: <u>Freight Train</u> by Donald Crews

Freight Train

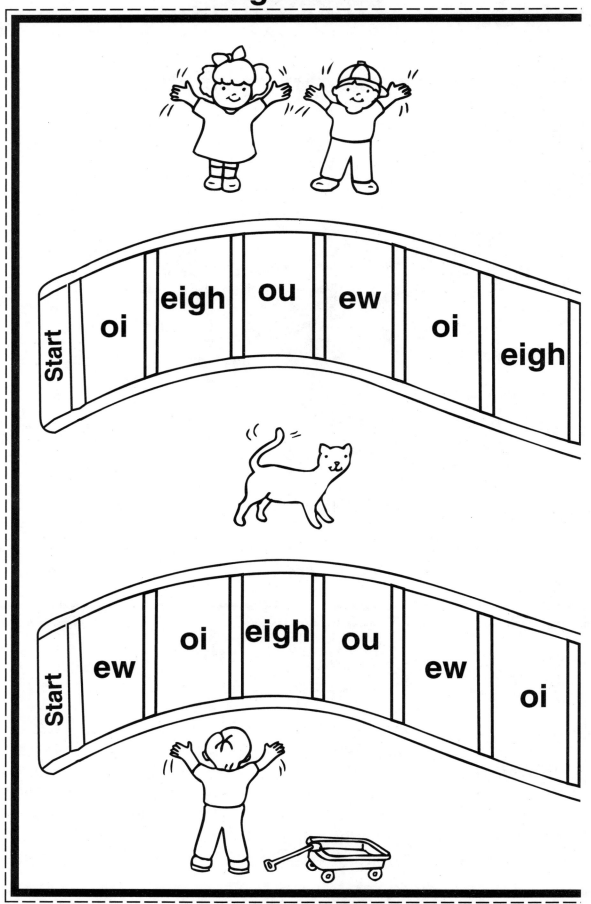

oi eigh ou ew oi eigh

Start

ew oi eigh ou ew oi

Start

Freight Train

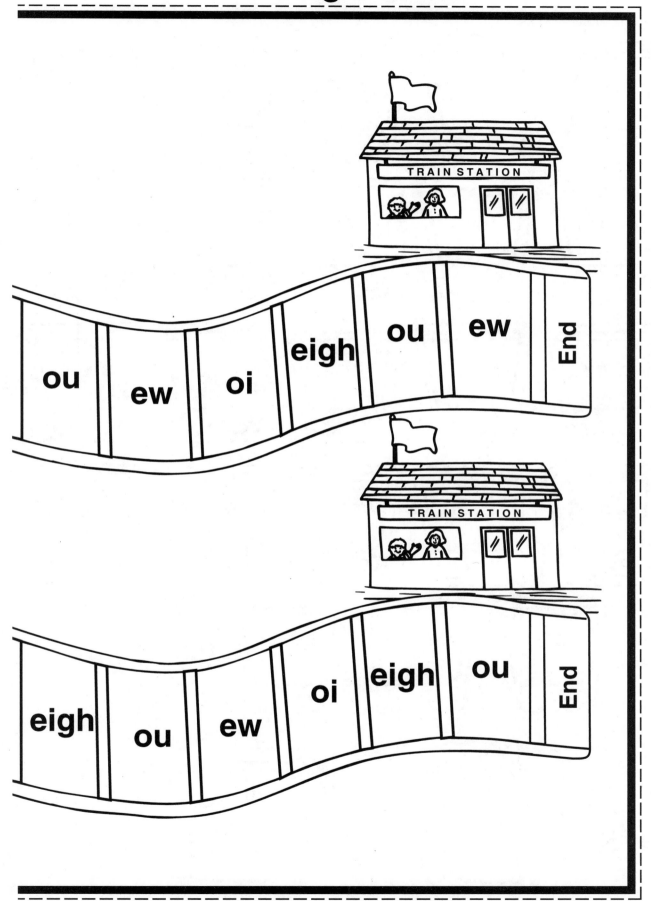

Freight Train

oil sleigh few out coin

neigh new loud moist freight

grew shout boil eight stew

proud broil weight drew round

hoist weigh crew mount

56

13

Wild Card Cricket Race

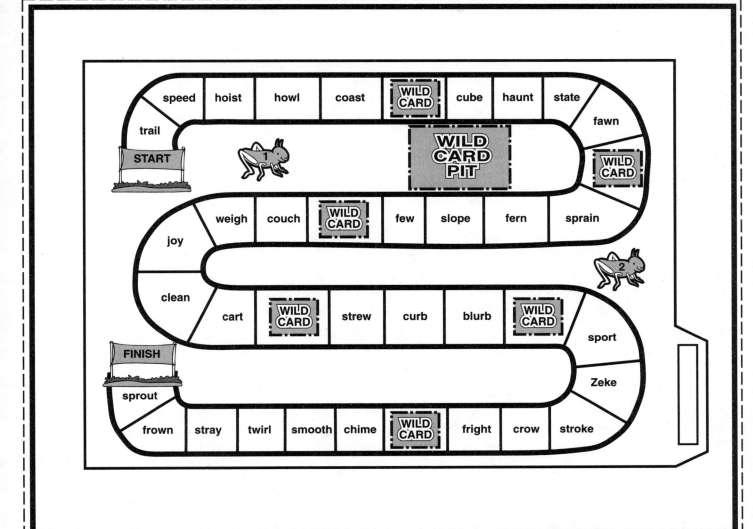

Wild Card Cricket Race

Phonograms/r-control

Directions: Three children may play. Take out the markers, the die, and the wild cards. Place the cards face down. Open the folder. Pick a cricket marker and place it on Start. Take turns throwing the die. Move your marker that number of places on the board. Read the word you land on. If you land on a wild card space, pick a wild card and follow the direction. The first player to reach Finish is the winner.

A book to read: <u>The Very Quiet Cricket</u> by Eric Carle

Wild Card Cricket Race

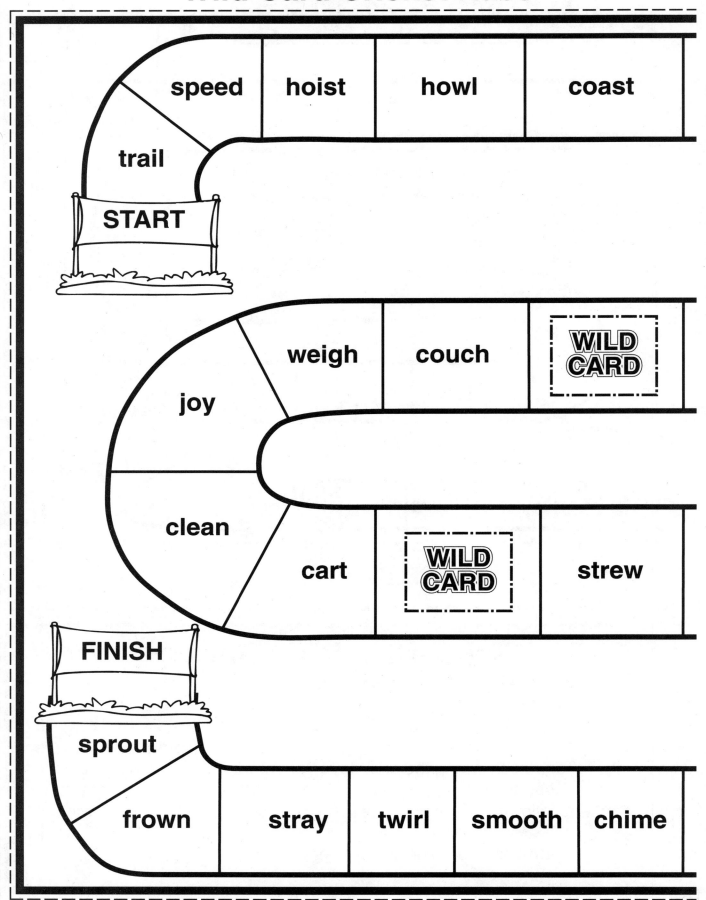

Wild Card Cricket Race

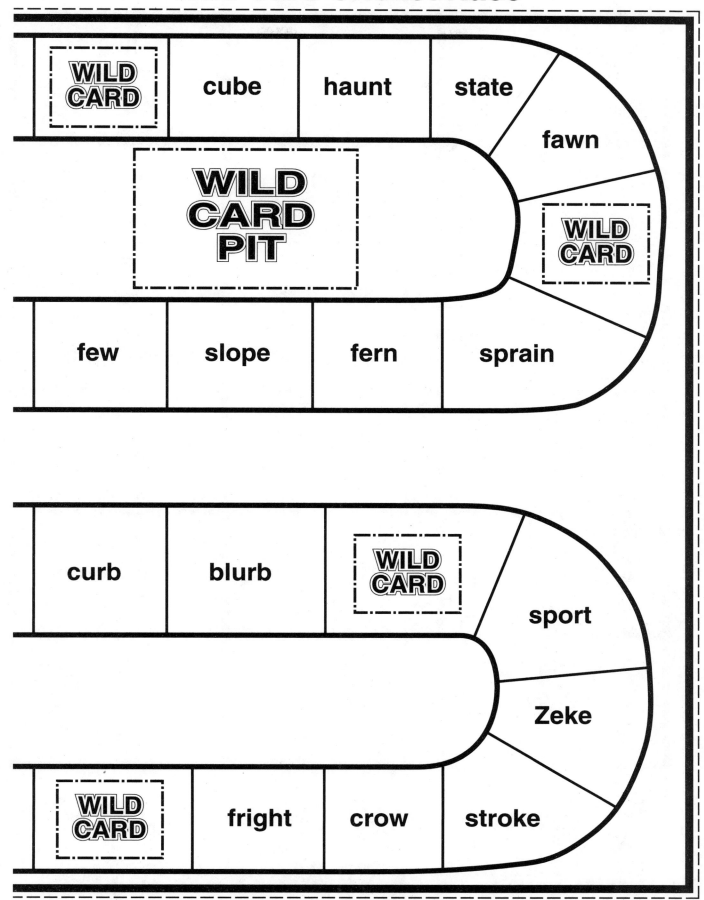

Wild Card Cricket Race

Name three words with ee, as in <u>feet</u>.	Go back two spaces.	Take one more turn.
Name two words with ar, as in <u>star</u>.	Skip two spaces.	Lose a turn.
Name three words with ay, as in <u>play</u>.	Go back one space.	Take one more turn.
Name two words with or, as in <u>corn</u>.	Skip one space.	Lose a turn.
Name three words with oo, as in <u>moon</u>.	Go back three spaces.	Read the last two words you passed.
Name two words with aw, as in <u>saw</u>.	Skip three spaces.	Read the last three words you passed.

14

Robot Maker

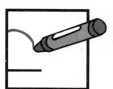

2.
Put one small half-circle on each side of the head.

1.
Draw one big eye at the top of the head and a line for a mouth.

Robot Maker

Directions

Directions: Two children may play. Take out the direction cards and mix them up. Place them face up. Open the folder and choose a robot and a felt pen. In turn, take a direction card, starting with number 1. Use a felt pen and follow that direction. The other player takes and follows the other number 1 direction card. Make your robot by following the directions in order.

A book to read: <u>Anatole and the Robot</u> by Eve Titius

Robot Maker

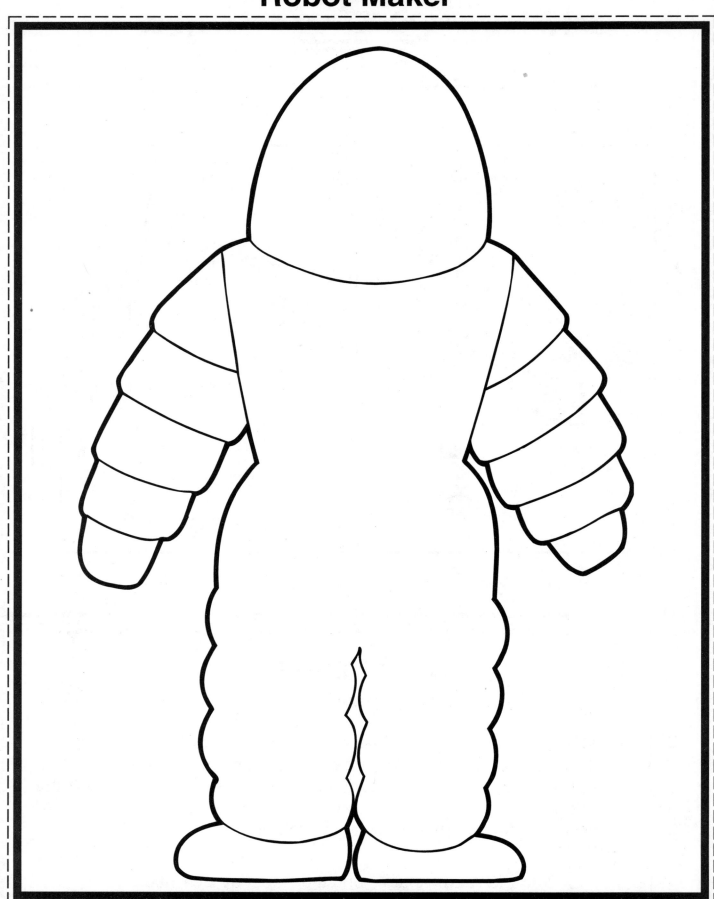

62

Robot Maker

Robot Maker

1. Draw one big eye at the top of the head and a line for a mouth.	**1.** Draw three small eyes in the center of the head and a large circle for a mouth.
2. Put two long feelers on each side of the head.	**2.** Put one small half-circle on each side of the head.
3. Make a large square shape on the top half of the body.	**3.** Make a large triangle in the middle of the robot's body.
4. Draw four buttons on the shape.	**4.** Draw a big star on the shape.
5. Make claw-like hands on the robot's arms.	**5.** Make mitten-like hands on the robot's arms.
6. Draw a walkie-talkie in one hand.	**6.** Draw a light stick in one of the robot's hands.
7. Draw two square pockets on each leg.	**7.** Draw one long pocket on each leg.
8. Draw roller skates on the robot's shoes.	**8.** Draw ice-skates on the robot's shoes.

15

Birthday Cake

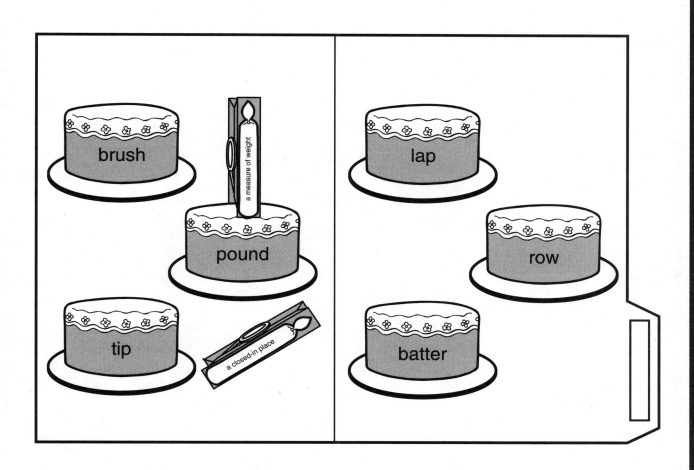

- brush
- pound *a measure of weight*
- tip
- *a closed-in place*
- lap
- row
- batter

Birthday Cake

Multiple word meanings

Directions: Two children may play. Take out the clothespins and place them face down. Open the folder and choose a set of three cakes. Read the words on the cakes. Take turns turning over a clothespin. If the meaning on it matches a word on one of your cakes, clip it to the cake. Find three meanings for each cake.

A book to read: <u>The World's Biggest Birthday Cake</u> by Carol Greene

Birthday Cake

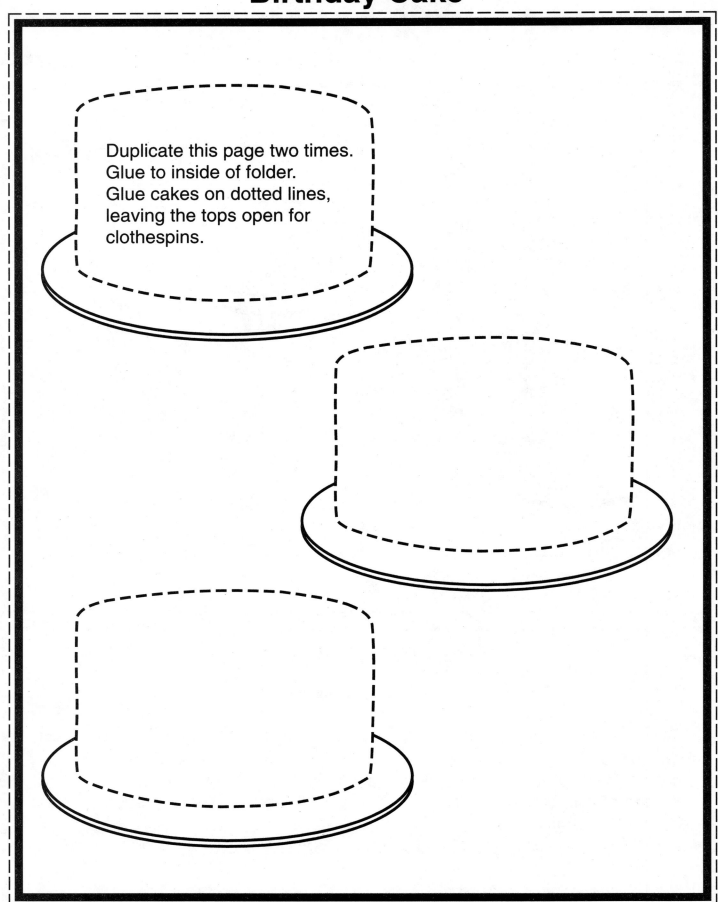

Duplicate this page two times.
Glue to inside of folder.
Glue cakes on dotted lines,
leaving the tops open for
clothespins.

Birthday Cake

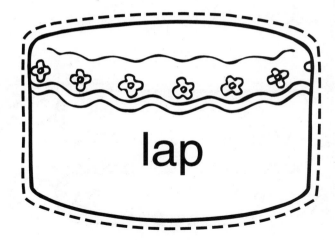

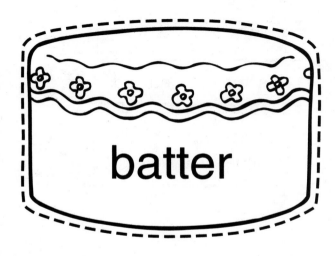

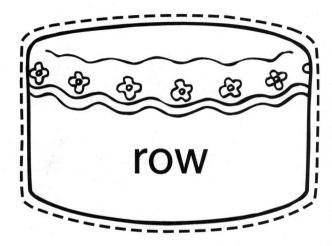

Birthday Cake

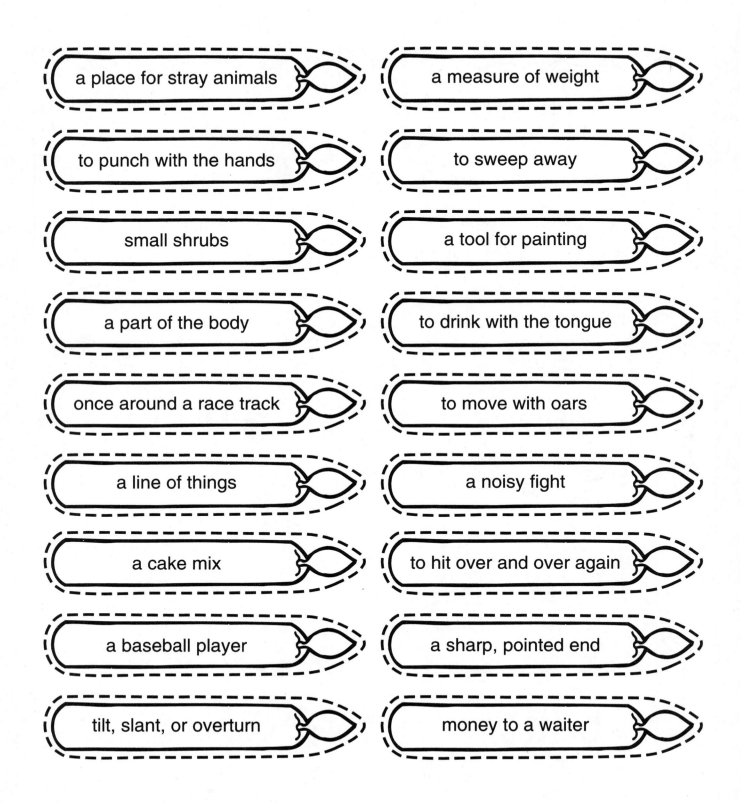

a place for stray animals

a measure of weight

to punch with the hands

to sweep away

small shrubs

a tool for painting

a part of the body

to drink with the tongue

once around a race track

to move with oars

a line of things

a noisy fight

a cake mix

to hit over and over again

a baseball player

a sharp, pointed end

tilt, slant, or overturn

money to a waiter

16

Up on a Cloud

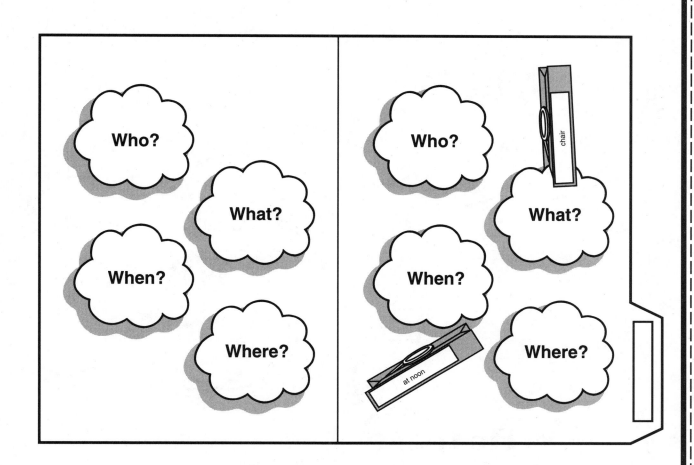

Up on a Cloud

Who, what, when, where

Directions: Two children may play. Take out the clothespins and place them face down. Open the folder and choose one side to play on. Pick a clothespin in turn. Read what it says. Check to see which question it answers and clip it to that cloud. The first player to put a clothespin on all of his or her clouds is the winner.

A book to read: <u>Jonathan's Cloud</u> by Gardner McFall

Up on a Cloud

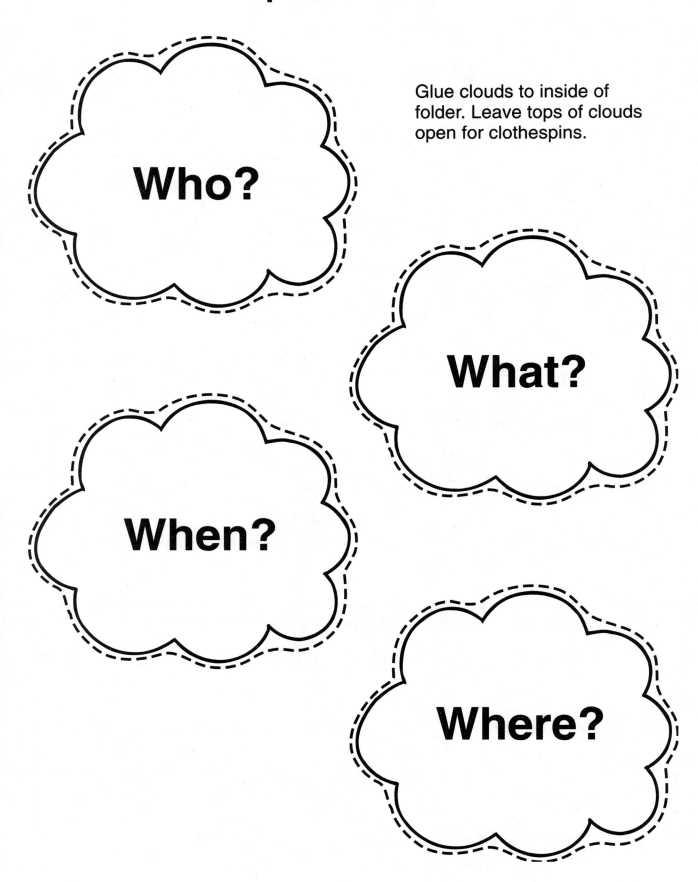

Glue clouds to inside of folder. Leave tops of clouds open for clothespins.

Who?

What?

When?

Where?

Up on a Cloud

Up on a Cloud

Tom	in the city
Carol	at the park
Mr. Peck	up high
Mrs. Lee	in the box
farmer	outside the house
teacher	in the sky
mother	from the school
clerk	to the station

chair	at noon
train	in the morning
farm	nine o'clock
store	one day
house	before school
clock	after lunch
food	in a minute
lizard	sometime

17

Sandwich It!

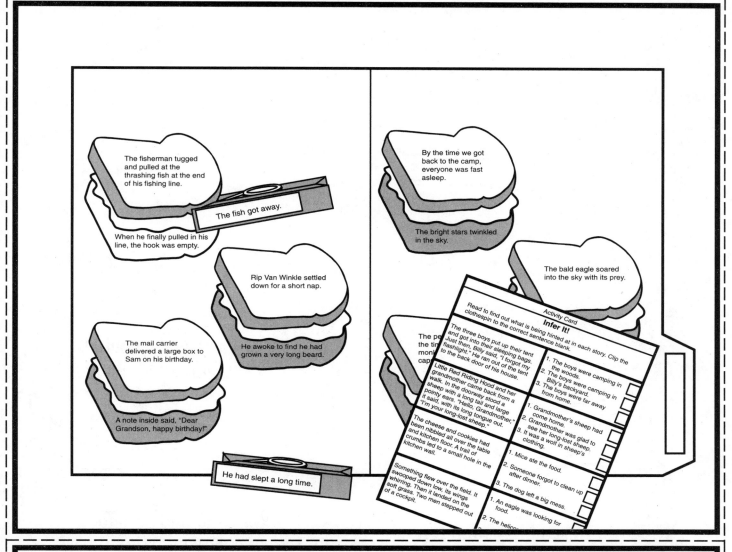

Sandwich It!

Reading between the lines

Directions: Take out the clothespins and the extra activity card. Place the clothespins face up. Leave out the four blank clothespins. Open the folder. Read what it says on the sandwiches. Pick a clothespin and read what it says. Clip it to the middle of the matching sandwich story. For the activity card, clip a blank clothespin to the sentence that is being hinted at.

A book to read: <u>The Giant Jam Sandwich</u> by John Vernon Lord

Sandwich It!

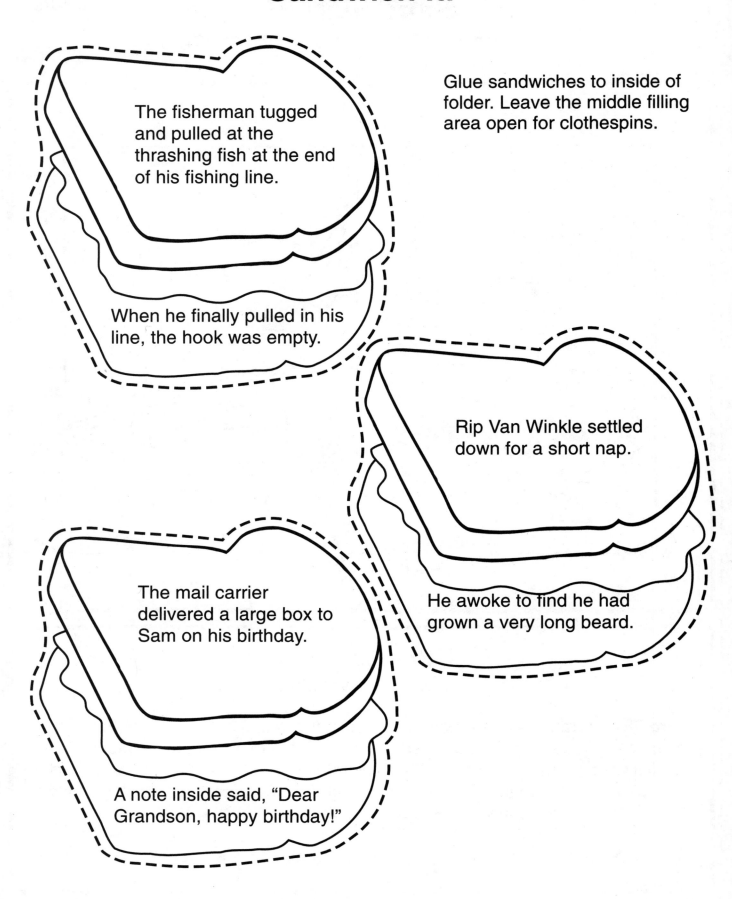

The fisherman tugged and pulled at the thrashing fish at the end of his fishing line.

When he finally pulled in his line, the hook was empty.

Glue sandwiches to inside of folder. Leave the middle filling area open for clothespins.

Rip Van Winkle settled down for a short nap.

He awoke to find he had grown a very long beard.

The mail carrier delivered a large box to Sam on his birthday.

A note inside said, "Dear Grandson, happy birthday!"

Sandwich It!

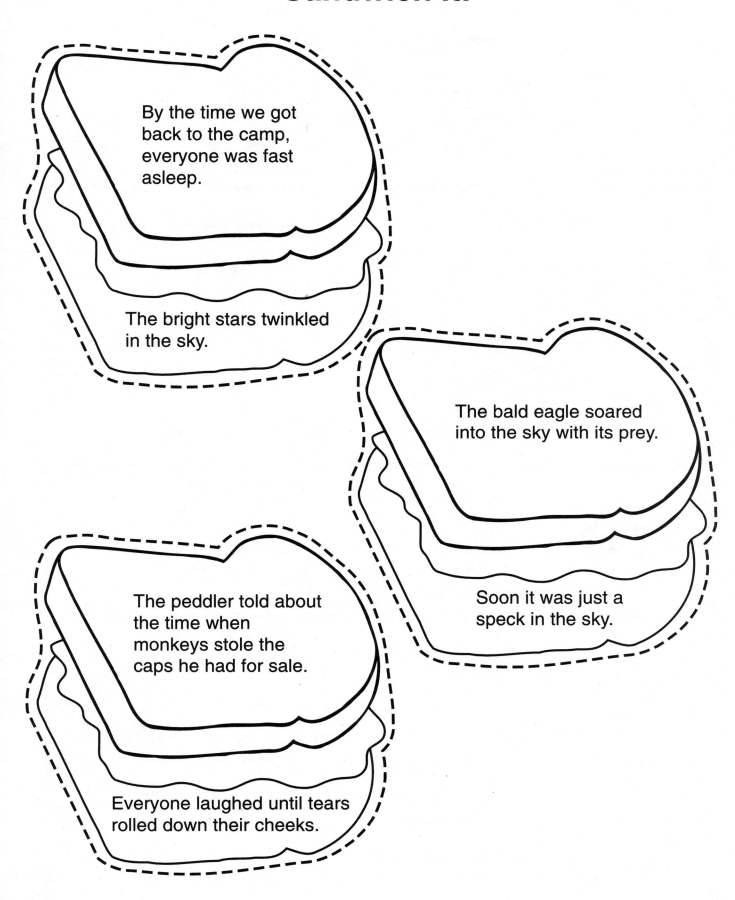

By the time we got back to the camp, everyone was fast asleep.

The bright stars twinkled in the sky.

The bald eagle soared into the sky with its prey.

Soon it was just a speck in the sky.

The peddler told about the time when monkeys stole the caps he had for sale.

Everyone laughed until tears rolled down their cheeks.

Sandwich It!

The fish got away.	It was night.
It was a present from Grandma.	It was far away.
He had slept a long time.	It was a funny story.

Activity Card

Infer It!

Read to find out what is being hinted at in each story. Clip the clothespin to the correct sentence blank.

The three boys put up their tent and got into their sleeping bags. Just then, Billy said, "I forgot my flashlight." He ran out of the tent to the back door of his house.	1. The boys were camping in the woods. ☐ 2. The boys were camping in Billy's backyard. ☐ 3. The boys were far away from home. ☐
Little Red Riding Hood and her grandmother came back from a walk. In the doorway stood a sheep with a long tail and large pointy ears. "Hello, Grandmother," it said, with its long tongue out. "I'm your long-lost sheep."	1. Grandmother's sheep had come home. ☐ 2. Grandmother was glad to see her long-lost sheep. ☐ 3. It was a wolf in sheep's clothing. ☐
The cheese and cookies had been nibbled all over the table and kitchen floor. A trail of crumbs led to a small hole in the kitchen wall.	1. Mice ate the food. ☐ 2. Someone forgot to clean up after dinner. ☐ 3. The dog left a big mess. ☐
Something flew over the field. It swooped down low, its wings whirring. Then it landed on the soft grass. Two men stepped out of a cockpit.	1. An eagle was looking for food. ☐ 2. The helicopter landed. ☐ 3. A butterfly landed on a bush. ☐

18

Witch's Brew

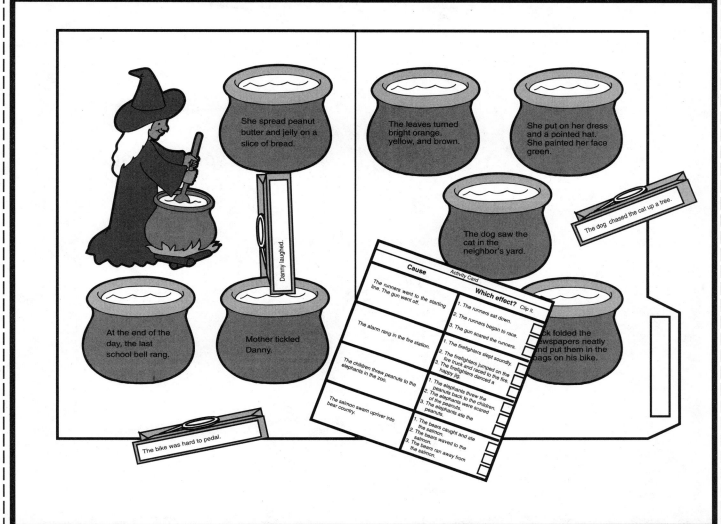

Witch's Brew

Cause and effect

Directions: Take out the clothespins and the activity card. Place the clothespins face up. Leave out the four blank pins. Open the folder. Read what is in the witch's pots—the causes. Take a clothespin and read what it says—an effect. Check to see which cause on one of the pots the effect matches. Match all the causes and effects. Next, pick up the activity card. Clip a blank clothespin on the correct effect for each cause.

A book to read: I Know I'm a Witch by David A. Adler

Witch's Brew

She spread peanut butter and jelly on a slice of bread.

Glue pots to inside of folder. Leave tops open for clothespins.

At the end of the day, the last school bell rang.

Mother tickled Danny.

Witch's Brew

The leaves turned bright orange, yellow, and brown.

She put on her dress and a pointed hat. She painted her face green.

The dog saw the cat in the neighbor's yard.

He hit the ball hard toward Mr. Anderson's house.

Jack folded the newspapers neatly and put them in the bags on his bike.

Witch's Brew

The children ran out of the school building.	She was a witch for Halloween.
She made a yummy sandwich.	The dog chased the cat up a tree.
Danny laughed.	The ball crashed through a window.
Soon the leaves fell off the trees.	The bike was hard to pedal.

Activity Card	
Cause	**Which effect?** Clip it.
The runners went to the starting line. The gun went off.	1. The runners sat down. ☐ 2. The runners began to race. ☐ 3. The gun scared the runners. ☐
The alarm rang in the fire station.	1. The firefighters slept soundly. ☐ 2. The firefighters jumped on the fire truck and raced to the fire. ☐ 3. The firefighters danced a happy jig. ☐
The children threw peanuts to the elephants in the zoo.	1. The elephants threw the peanuts back to the children. ☐ 2. The elephants were scared of the peanuts. ☐ 3. The elephants ate the peanuts. ☐
The salmon swam upriver into bear country.	1. The bears caught and ate the salmon. ☐ 2. The bears waved to the salmon. ☐ 3. The bears ran away from the salmon. ☐

19

Ostrich Feathers

Ostrich Feathers

Figurative expressions

Directions: Take out the clothespins and place them face up. Open the folder. Read what it says on the ostriches. Each set of words is the first part of an expression. Pick a clothespin in turn and read what it says. Clip it on the ostrich whose expression it finishes. Finish all the expressions with three clothespins each.

A book to read: <u>Lion and the Ostrich Chicks and Other African Tales</u> retold by Ashley Bryan

Ostrich Feathers

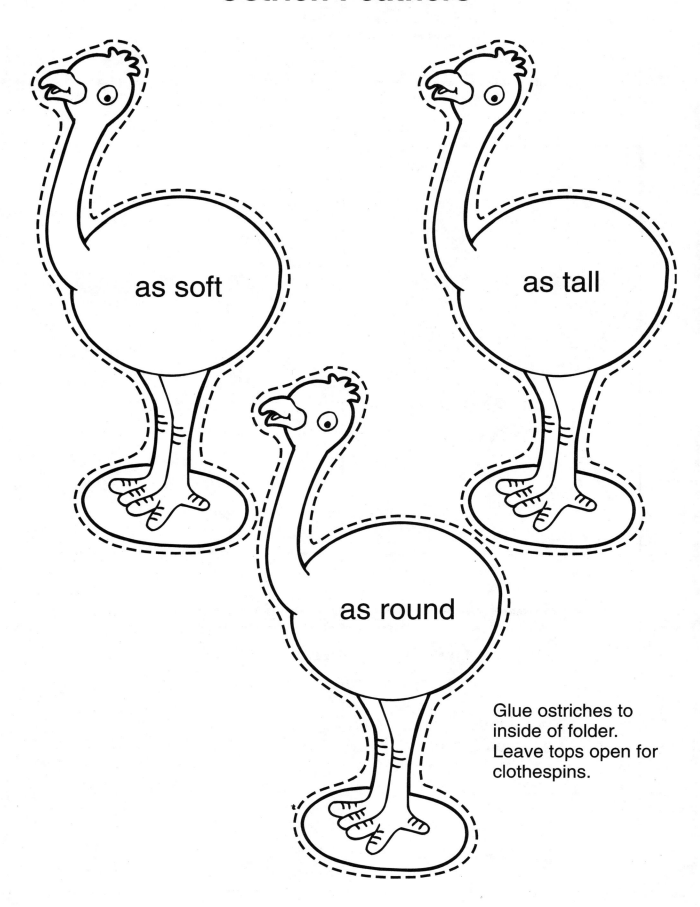

as soft

as tall

as round

Glue ostriches to
inside of folder.
Leave tops open for
clothespins.

Ostrich Feathers

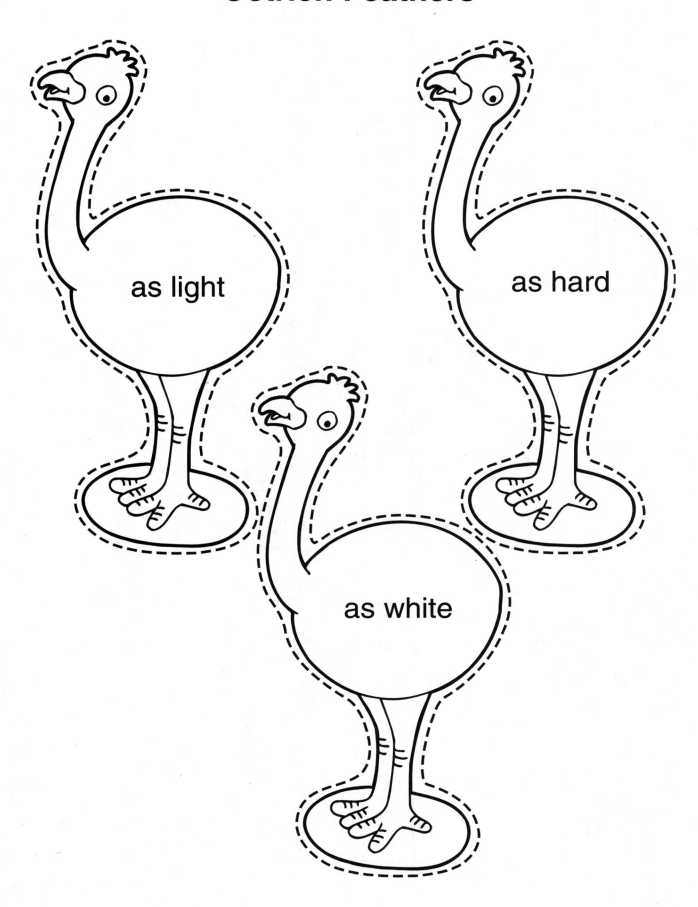

as light

as hard

as white

Ostrich Feathers

as a feather

as air

as a pin

as a rock

as a nut

as metal

as snow

as a sheet

as a cloud

as a pillow

as a baby

as cotton

as a skyscraper

as a giraffe

as a steeple

as a ball

as the moon

as a marble

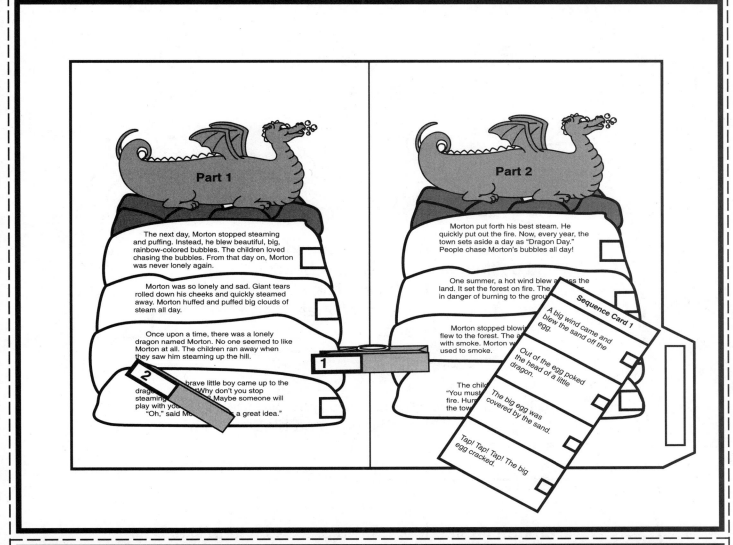

Dragon Power
Sequence of events

Directions: Two children may play. Take out the clothespins and the sequence activity cards. Place the clothespins face up with the numbers showing. Open the folder. Read together the mixed-up story about the dragon in Part 1. Correct the story order by pinning clothespins to parts in the correct order—1, 2, 3, 4. Read to check. Do the same for Part 2. Then reread the whole story, parts 1 and 2, to double-check the order. Next, take out the activity cards. Put the story parts in order by clipping on the numbered clothespins.

A book to read: Demi's Dragons and Fantastic Creatures by Demi

Dragon Power

Part 1

The next day, Morton stopped steaming and puffing. Instead, he blew beautiful, big, rainbow-colored bubbles. The children loved chasing the bubbles. From that day on, Morton was never lonely again.

Morton was so lonely and sad. Giant tears rolled down his cheeks and quickly steamed away. Morton huffed and puffed big clouds of steam all day.

Once upon a time, there was a lonely dragon named Morton. No one seemed to like Morton at all. The children ran away when they saw him steaming up the hill.

One day, a brave little boy came up to the dragon and said, "Why don't you stop steaming and puffing? Maybe someone will play with you."
"Oh," said Morton. "That's a great idea."

Cut on dotted line. Glue to inside of folder.
Leave right side open for clothespins.

Dragon Power

Part 2

Morton put forth his best steam. He quickly put out the fire. Now, every year, the town sets aside a day as "Dragon Day." People chase Morton's bubbles all day!

One summer, a hot wind blew across the land. It set the forest on fire. The town was in danger of burning to the ground.

Morton stopped blowing his bubbles. He flew to the forest. The air was hot and filled with smoke. Morton was not afraid! He was used to smoke.

The children ran to Morton and said, "You must come and help us put out the fire. Hurry, Morton! The fire is coming to the town!"

Cut on dotted line. Glue to inside of folder. Leave right side open for clothespins.

Dragon Power

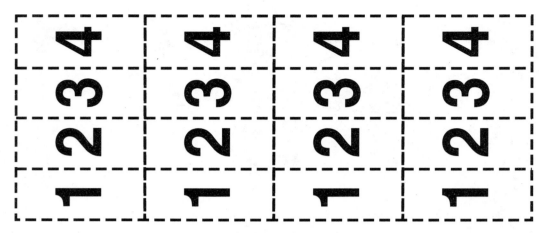

Activity Cards

Sequence Card 1	Sequence Card 2
A big wind came and blew the sand off the egg. ☐	Little Dragon found a cave on the hillside that was just right. ☐
Out of the egg poked the head of a little dragon. ☐	Little Dragon looked for a good den. ☐
The big egg was covered by the sand. ☐	Tired Little Dragon settled down for a good dragon nap. ☐
Tap! Tap! Tap! The big egg cracked. ☐	Little Dragon hopped out of the egg. ☐

21

Seal Pups

Seal Pups

Main idea

Directions: Take out the clothespins and the activity card. Place the clothespins face up. Leave out the blank ones. Open the folder. Read the story details on the seals. Take a main idea clothespin and read what it says. Clip it to the matching seal's ball. Match all the main ideas. Next, take the activity card. Clip a blank clothespin to the main idea for each story.

A book to read: <u>Sammy the Seal</u> by Syd Hoff

Seal Pups

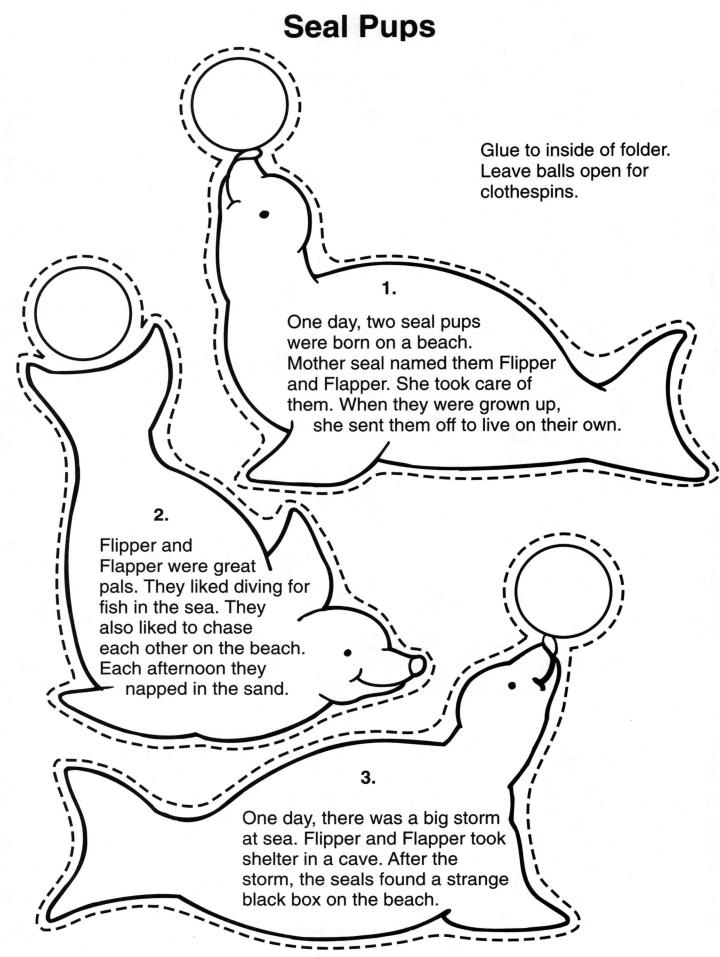

Glue to inside of folder. Leave balls open for clothespins.

1.

One day, two seal pups were born on a beach. Mother seal named them Flipper and Flapper. She took care of them. When they were grown up, she sent them off to live on their own.

2.

Flipper and Flapper were great pals. They liked diving for fish in the sea. They also liked to chase each other on the beach. Each afternoon they napped in the sand.

3.

One day, there was a big storm at sea. Flipper and Flapper took shelter in a cave. After the storm, the seals found a strange black box on the beach.

Seal Pups

4.

In the box, Flipper and Flapper discovered an old treasure map. The map told of a buried treasure on a small nearby island.

5.

Flipper and Flapper swam to the island. They followed the clues on the map and found the treasure. It was a trunk filled with coins, jewels, swords, and pirates' clothing.

6.

Flipper and Flapper took the treasure back to the cave. They counted the coins. They put the jewels around the cave to make it sparkle. Best of all, they dressed up and stomped around like pirates! The End.

Seal Pups

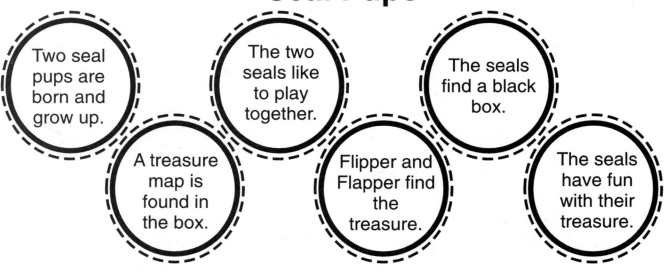

- Two seal pups are born and grow up.
- The two seals like to play together.
- The seals find a black box.
- A treasure map is found in the box.
- Flipper and Flapper find the treasure.
- The seals have fun with their treasure.

Glue circles onto oak tag. Cut out and glue on clothespins.

Activity Card
What's the Main Idea?

Joan and Nick made the people on the screen chase each other. Click, click, click! Faster and faster! Finally, Joan's man fell into a trap. Nick won the game.	1. Joan and Nick like to play hopscotch. ☐ 2. Joan and Nick are playing a video game. ☐ 3. Joan and Nick like to chase each other. ☐
The clerk put the milk carton in the bag. Next, he added the cans of soup. Finally, he placed the vegetables in the bag. We paid for our groceries and went home.	1. The groceries were bagged. ☐ 2. The clerk was a man. ☐ 3. We like to drink milk. ☐
The house was dark. Then the lights came back on. The refrigerator hummed. The clock flashed "reset." We blew out the candles.	1. We were scared of the dark. ☐ 2. The electricity came back on. ☐ 3. It was a dark and stormy night. ☐
The bird sat on her nest. She kept her eggs warm. She waited for the eggs to hatch. Finally, she heard a "peep," and her first chick broke its shell.	1. A baby bird hatches from an egg. ☐ 2. An ugly duckling is born. ☐ 3. Birds say, "Peep." ☐

22

Eager Beavers

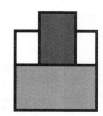

Eager Beavers

Supporting details

Directions: Two children may play. Take out the slip-in logs and place them face up. Open the folder. Read the main idea sentence on the first dam. Find a log that matches the main idea. Slip it into the slit in the log. Do the same for the other detail logs. Put them in the right order on the dam. The size of the logs will help you. Do this until all the matches are made. Reread to check.

A book to read: <u>Fun in the Sun</u> by Ski Michaels

Eager Beavers

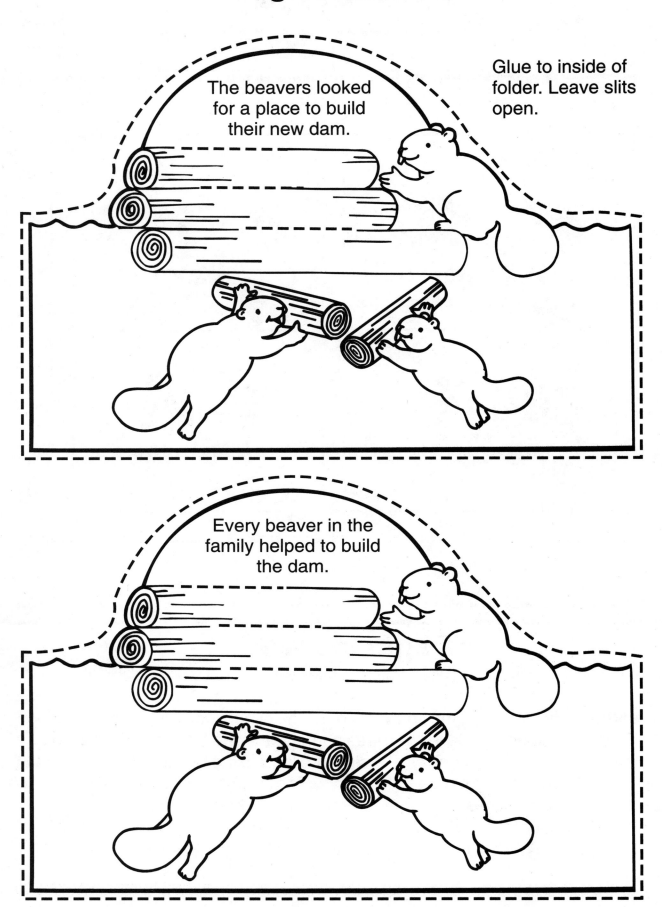

The beavers looked for a place to build their new dam.

Glue to inside of folder. Leave slits open.

Every beaver in the family helped to build the dam.

Eager Beavers

After the dam was built, the beavers played and relaxed.

The dam was a cozy and snug den for the beavers.

Eager Beavers

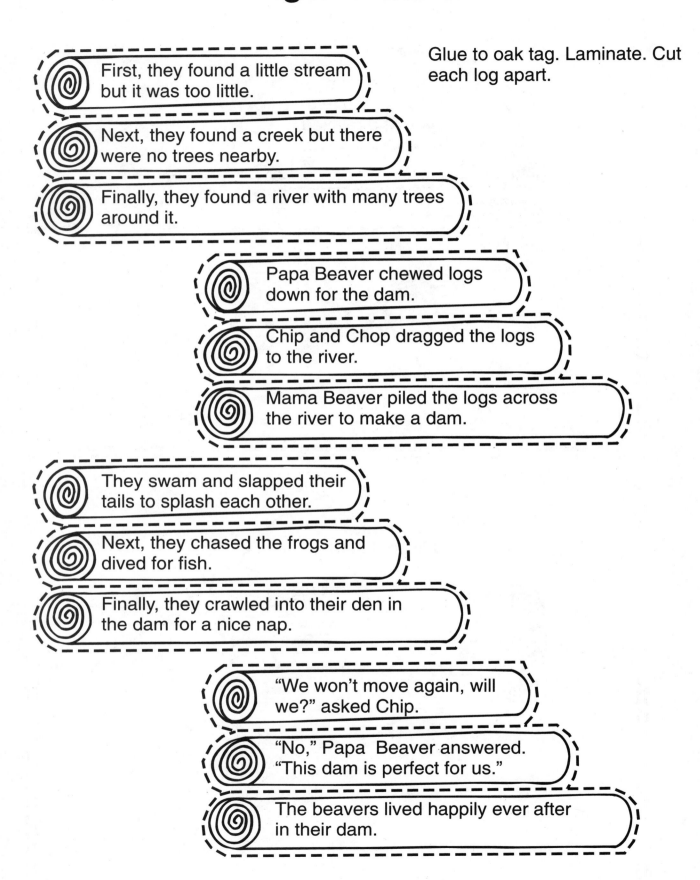

Glue to oak tag. Laminate. Cut each log apart.

First, they found a little stream but it was too little.

Next, they found a creek but there were no trees nearby.

Finally, they found a river with many trees around it.

Papa Beaver chewed logs down for the dam.

Chip and Chop dragged the logs to the river.

Mama Beaver piled the logs across the river to make a dam.

They swam and slapped their tails to splash each other.

Next, they chased the frogs and dived for fish.

Finally, they crawled into their den in the dam for a nice nap.

"We won't move again, will we?" asked Chip.

"No," Papa Beaver answered. "This dam is perfect for us."

The beavers lived happily ever after in their dam.

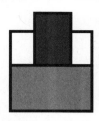

The monkeys swung from tree to tree with their long legs and strong arms. They plucked fruit while hanging by their tails. They even formed monkey chains to cross a river.

Jim helped his family get things ready for a picnic in the park. He packed the car with food and toys. Everyone piled into the car. Just then it started to rain heavily.

Ted ran up to Kim and tagged her. "You're it!" he shouted. Kim chased after Tom and tagged him. "Now, you're it," she said happily. Tom ran after Mary, but Mary got away.

The children played a game of tag.

Lisa put the film in the camera. She looked through the lens. She held the camera steady and pressed the button. Click!

The lights went off. The theater was dark. Then the curtains opened and the movie started. ...ared her popcorn with ...Everyone was happy.

...smart dog who ...many things.

Toby, the toy poodle, danced and twirled on his hind legs. He could jump through a hoop and do other tricks. He could even add by barking out the answers.

Treasure Boxes

Conclusions

Directions: Two children may play. Take out the treasure box conclusion cards. Place them face up. Open the folder. Read the stories on the treasure boxes. Pick a card and read the conclusion. Find the conclusion that matches a story on each of the treasure boxes. Slip it into the correct slot. Do this until all the conclusion matches are made.

A book to read: <u>Gorman and the Treasure Chest</u> by John Stadler

Treasure Boxes

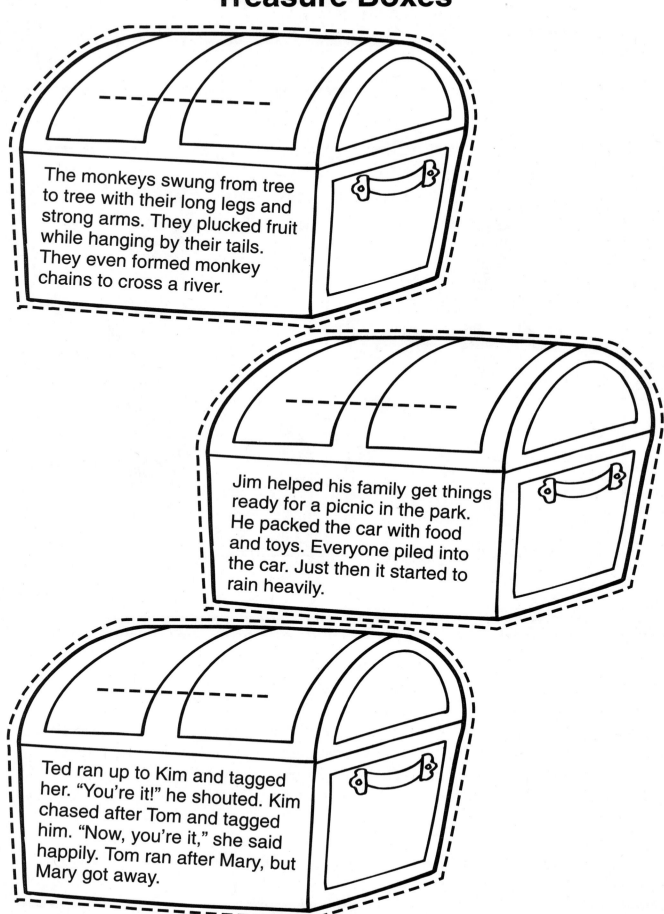

The monkeys swung from tree to tree with their long legs and strong arms. They plucked fruit while hanging by their tails. They even formed monkey chains to cross a river.

Jim helped his family get things ready for a picnic in the park. He packed the car with food and toys. Everyone piled into the car. Just then it started to rain heavily.

Ted ran up to Kim and tagged her. "You're it!" he shouted. Kim chased after Tom and tagged him. "Now, you're it," she said happily. Tom ran after Mary, but Mary got away.

Treasure Boxes

- - - - - - - - - - - - - - -

Lisa put the film in the camera. She looked through the lens. She held the camera steady and pressed the button. Click!

- - - - - - - - - - - - - - -

The lights went off. The theater was dark. Then the curtains opened and the movie started. Jane shared her popcorn with José. Everyone was happy.

- - - - - - - - - - - - - - -

Toby, the toy poodle, danced and twirled on his hind legs. He could jump through a hoop and do other tricks. He could even add by barking out the answers.

Treasure Boxes

The monkeys used their bodies well to get around.

Lisa took a picture with her camera.

It wasn't a good day for a picnic in the park.

Jane and José had fun at the movies.

The children played a game of tag.

Toby is a smart dog who can do many things.

24

Possum on Board

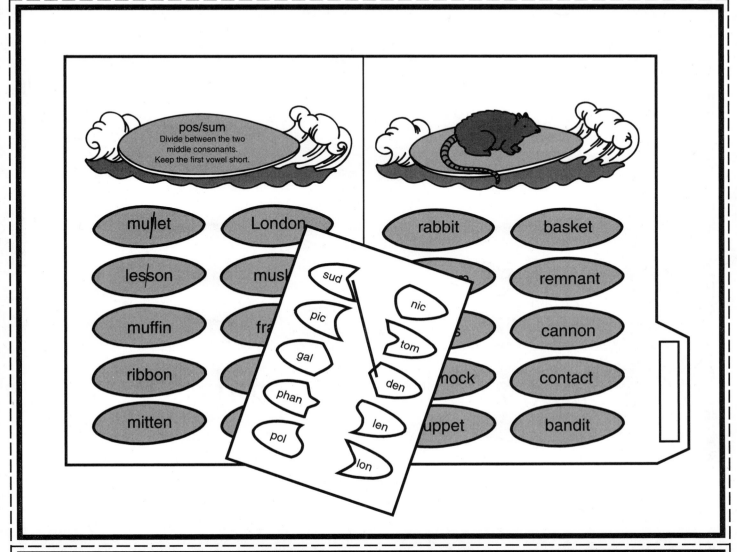

pos/sum
Divide between the two
middle consonants.
Keep the first vowel short.

mullet

lesson

muffin

ribbon

mitten

London

musk

fra

rabbit

basket

remnant

cannon

contact

bandit

nock

uppet

sud

nic

pic

tom

gal

den

phan

len

pol

lon

Possum on Board

Dividing between the two middle consonants

Directions: Take out the felt pen or erasable crayon and the activity cards. Open the folder. Read the directions on the big surfboard. Use the felt pen or crayon to divide the words on the smaller surfboards. Divide between the two consonants. Check the sample. For the activity cards, use the felt pen or crayon to connect the syllables that go together. Have your work checked. Wipe off the folder and cards with a soft tissue or rag.

A book to read: Possum Magic by Mem Fox

Possum on Board

pos/sum
Divide between the two middle consonants.
Keep the first vowel short.

mullet

London

lesson

musket

muffin

frantic

ribbon

piston

mitten

candid

Possum on Board

rabbit

basket

blossom

remnant

tennis

cannon

hammock

contact

puppet

bandit

Possum on Board

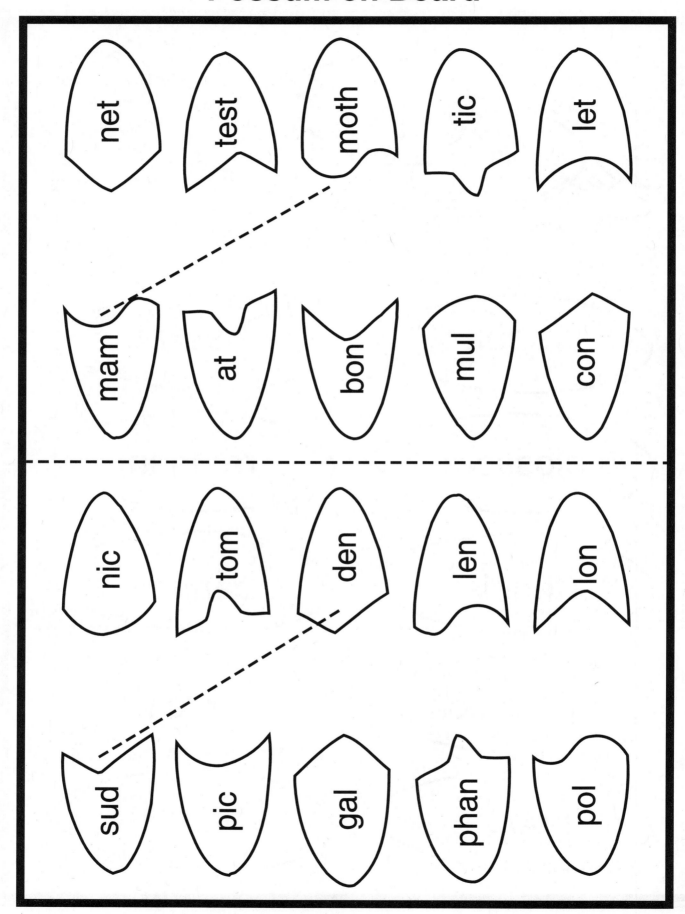

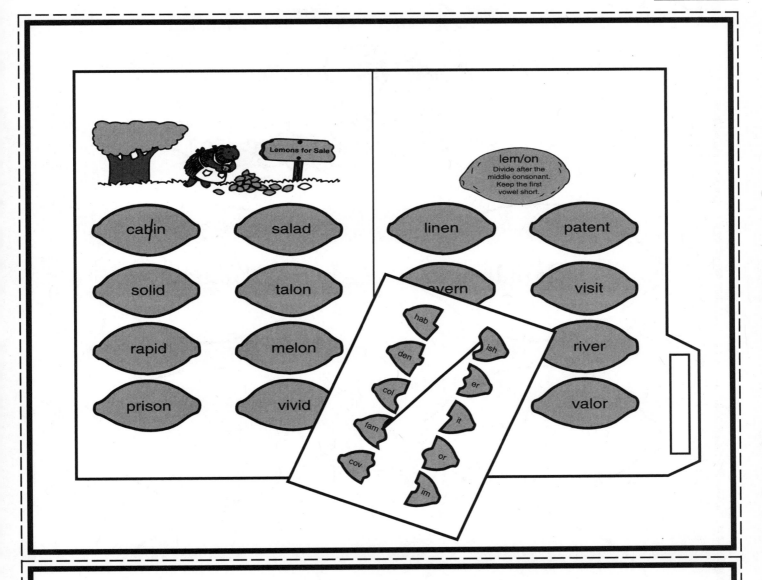

25

Hedgehog's Lemons

Dividing after the middle consonant

Directions: Take out the felt pen or erasable crayon and the activity cards. Open the folder. Read the directions on Hedgehog's lemon. Use the felt pen or crayon to divide the words on the lemons. Divide after the middle consonant to keep the first vowel short. Check the sample. For the activity cards, use the felt pen or crayon to connect the syllables that go together. Have your work checked. Wipe off the folder and cards with a soft tissue or rag.

A book to read: The Happy Hedgehog Band by Jill Barton

Hedgehog's Lemons

Lemons for Sale

cabin

salad

solid

talon

rapid

melon

prison

vivid

Hedgehog's Lemons

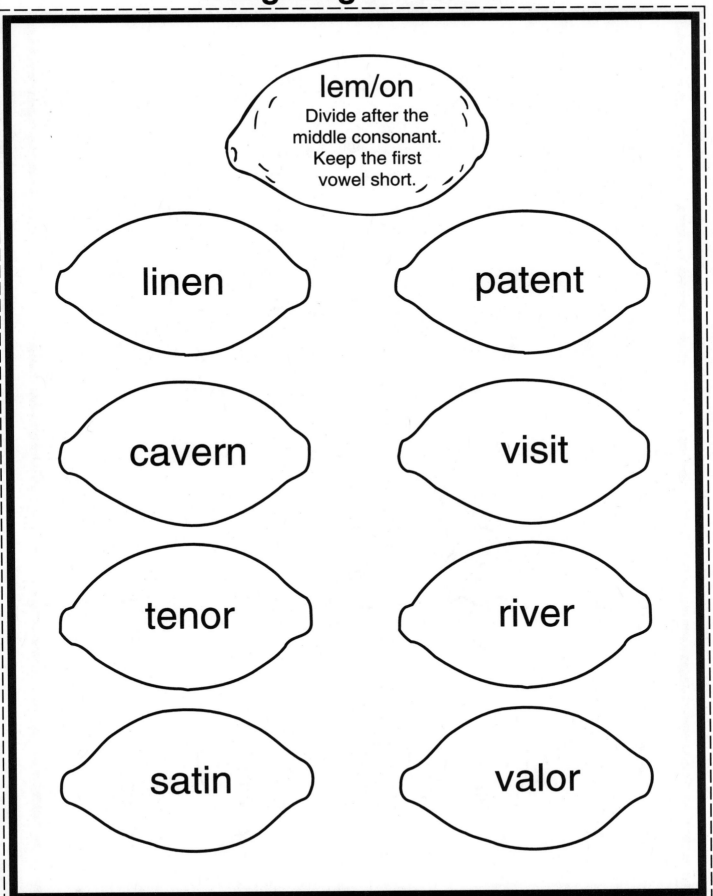

lem/on
Divide after the
middle consonant.
Keep the first
vowel short.

linen

patent

cavern

visit

tenor

river

satin

valor

Hedgehog's Lemons

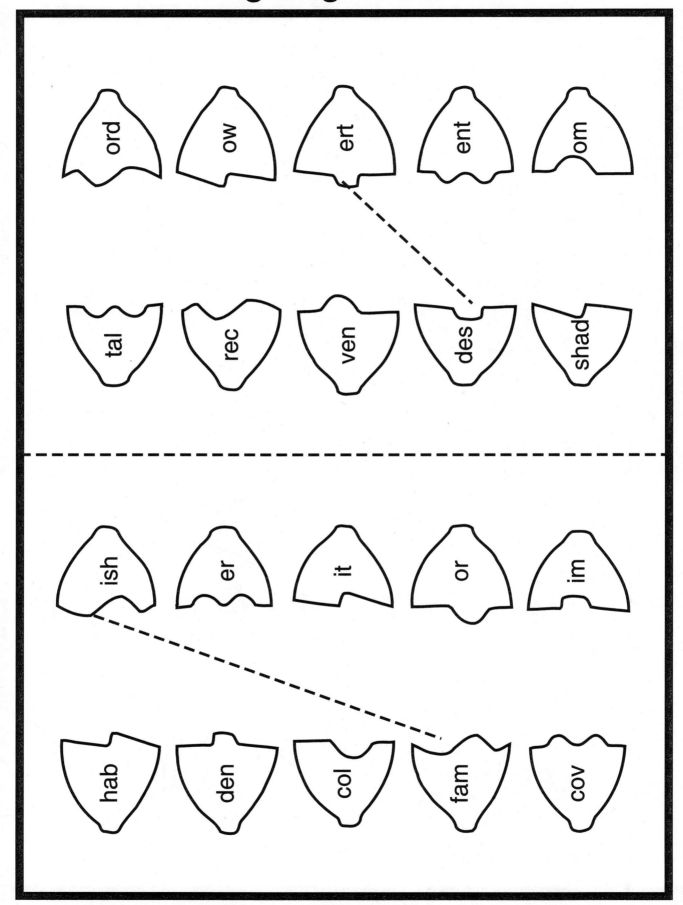

26

Pirate Ship

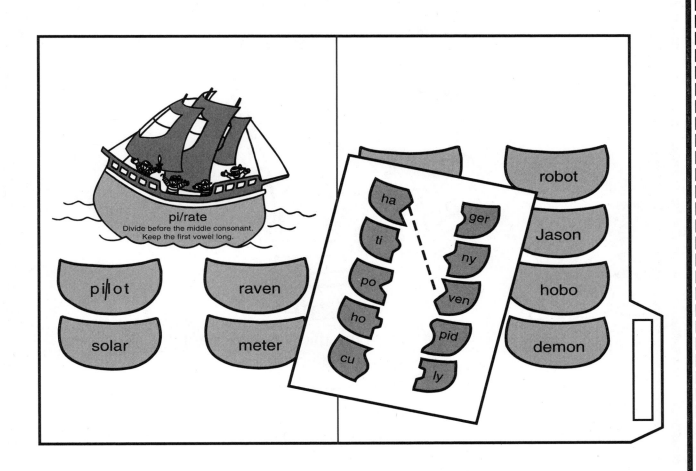

pi/rate
Divide before the middle consonant.
Keep the first vowel long.

pi|lot

raven

solar

meter

robot

Jason

hobo

demon

ha
ti
po
ho
cu

ger
ny
ven
pid
ly

Pirate Ship

Dividing before the middle consonant

Directions: Take out the felt pen or erasable crayon and the activity cards. Open the folder. Read the directions on the pirate ship. Use the felt pen or crayon to divide the words on the boats. Divide before the middle consonant to keep the first vowel long. Check the sample. For the activity cards, use the felt pen or crayon to connect the syllables that go together.

A book to read: I Wish I Had a Pirate Suit by Pamela Allen

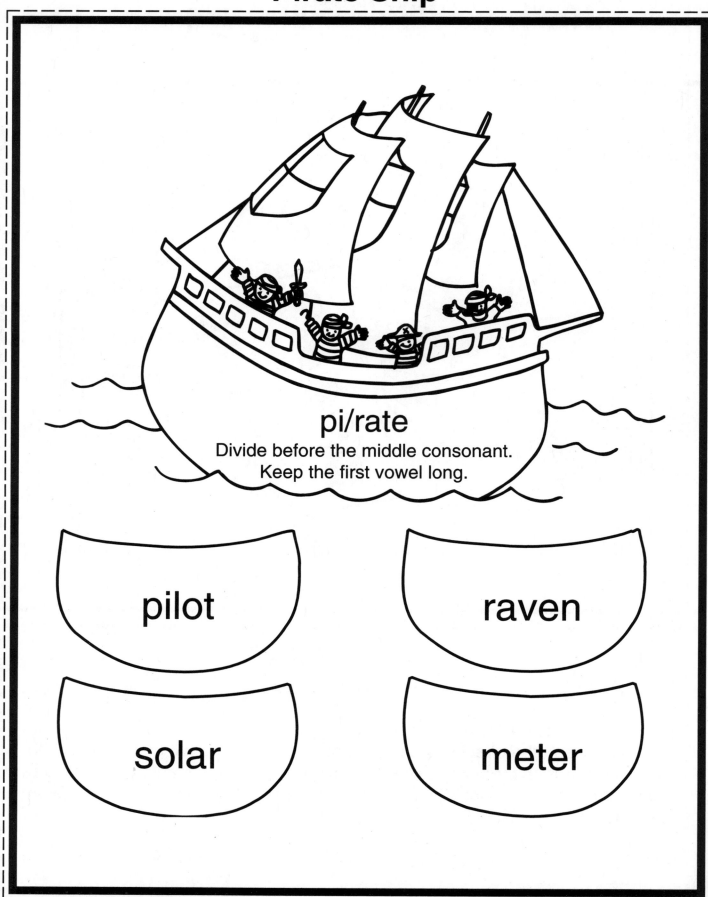

pi/rate
Divide before the middle consonant.
Keep the first vowel long.

pilot

raven

solar

meter

Pirate Ship

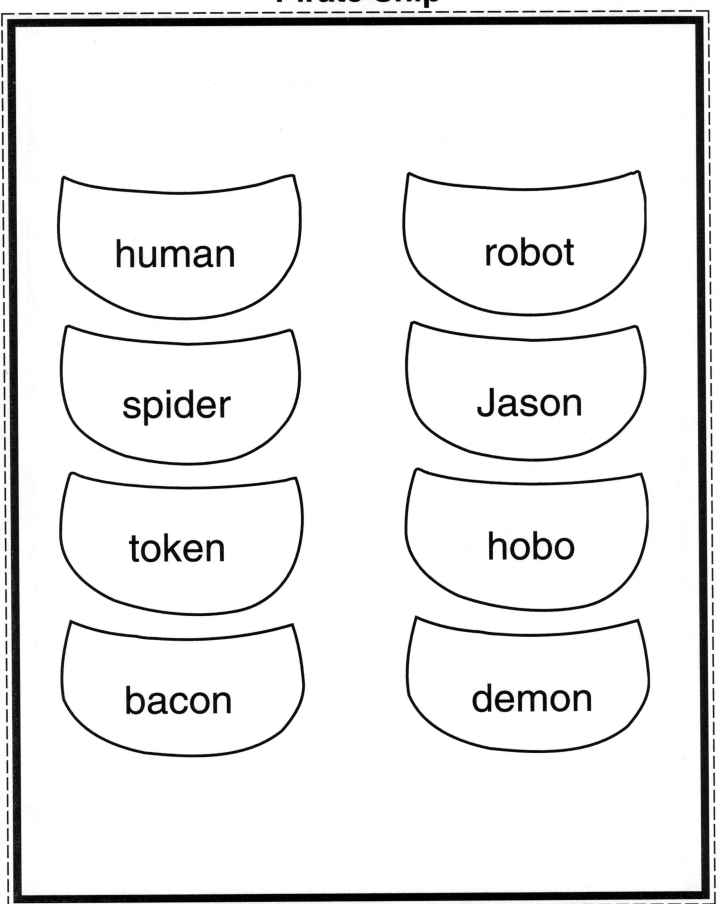

human

robot

spider

Jason

token

hobo

bacon

demon

111

Pirate Ship

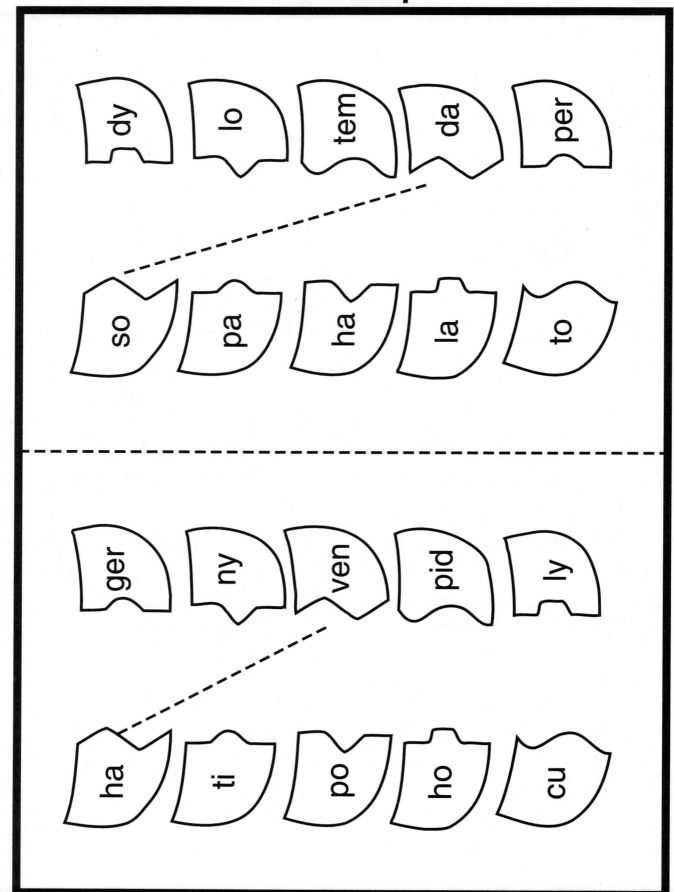

27

Poodles and Noodles

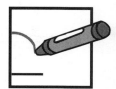

Poodles and Noodles

Dividing before the consonant-le syllable

Directions: Take out the felt pen or erasable crayon and the activity cards. Open the folder. Read the directions on the noodles. Use the felt pen or crayon to divide the words on the noodles. Divide before the consonant-le syllable. Check the sample. For the activity cards, use the felt pen or crayon to connect the syllables that go together. Have your work checked. Wipe off the folder and cards with a soft tissue or rag.

A book to read: Anatole and the Poodle by Eve Titus

Poodles and Noodles

poo/dle
Divide before the consonant-le syllable.
Keep the consonant-le together.

noodle

muzzle

little

cradle

sample

steeple

Poodles and Noodles

fiddle

purple

hurdle

candle

wiggle

shuttle

twinkle

jungle

needle

tackle

Poodles and Noodles

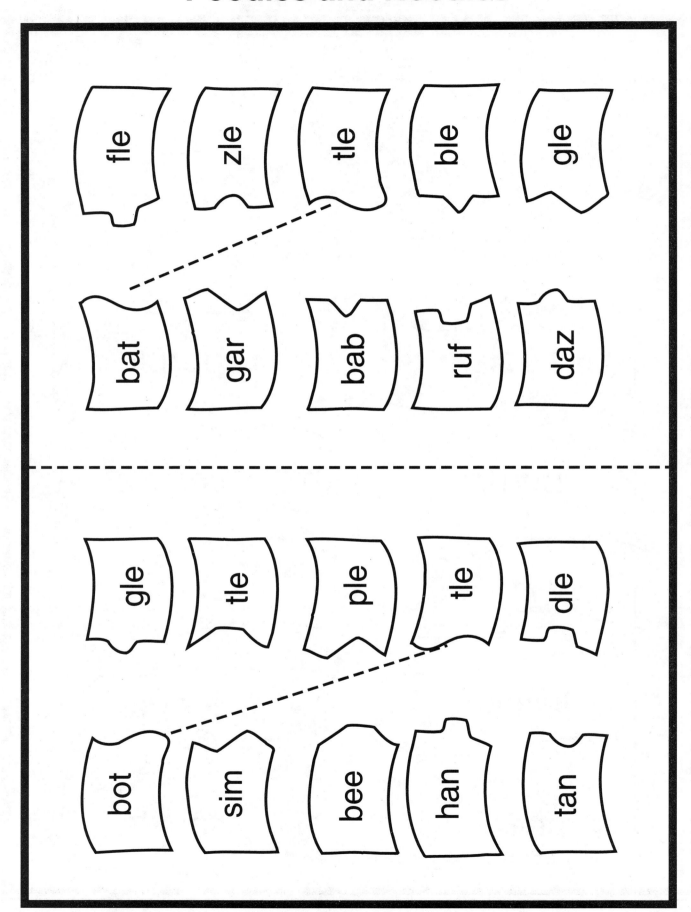

116

28. | Lizards' Tails

Lizards' Tails

Suffixes

Directions: Two children may play. Take out the clothespins, felt pen or crayon, and the activity cards. Place the clothespins face down. Open the folder. Choose a side to play on. Pick a clothespin in turn. Check to see if the suffix matches a word on a lizard. If it does, clip it to the lizard. If it doesn't, put it back. See who can clip on all his or her lizards' tails first. For the activity cards, write a base word for each suffix. Have your work checked. Wipe off the activity card with a soft tissue or rag.

A book to read: <u>Lizard in the Sun</u> by Joanna Ryder

Lizards' Tails

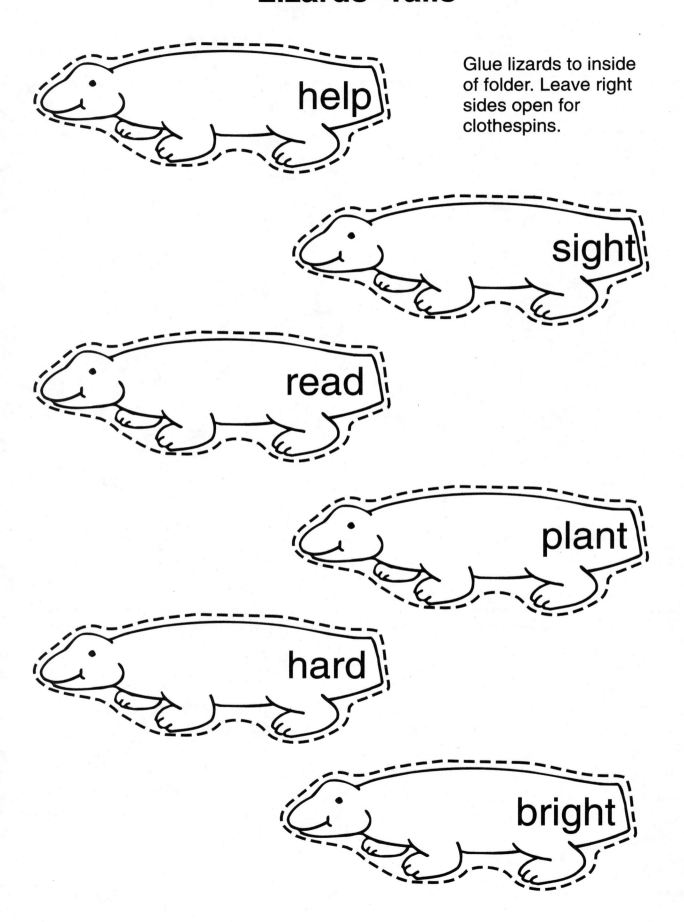

Glue lizards to inside of folder. Leave right sides open for clothespins.

help

sight

read

plant

hard

bright

Lizards' Tails

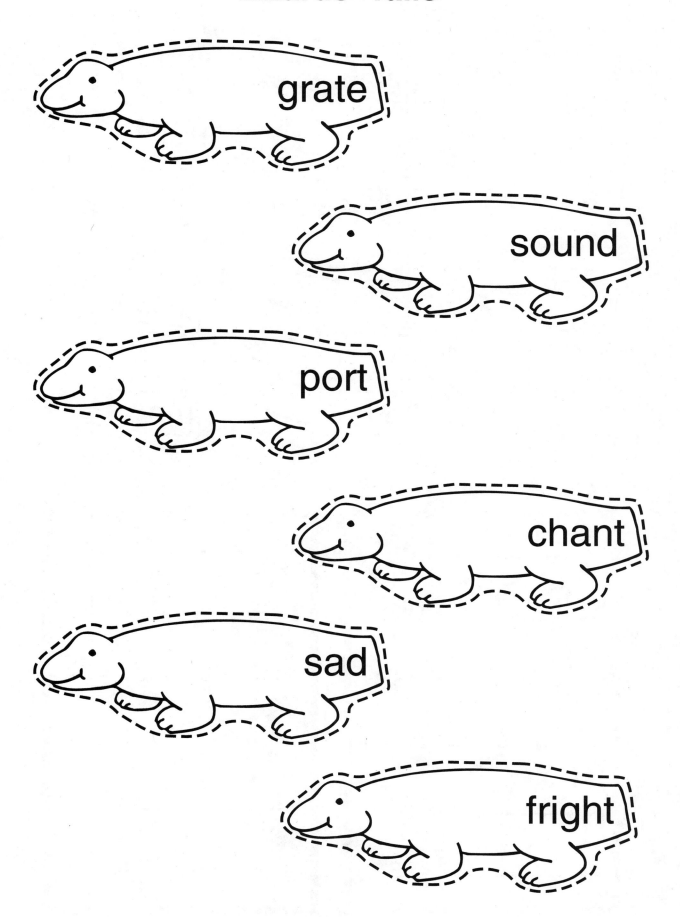

grate

sound

port

chant

sad

fright

Lizards' Tails

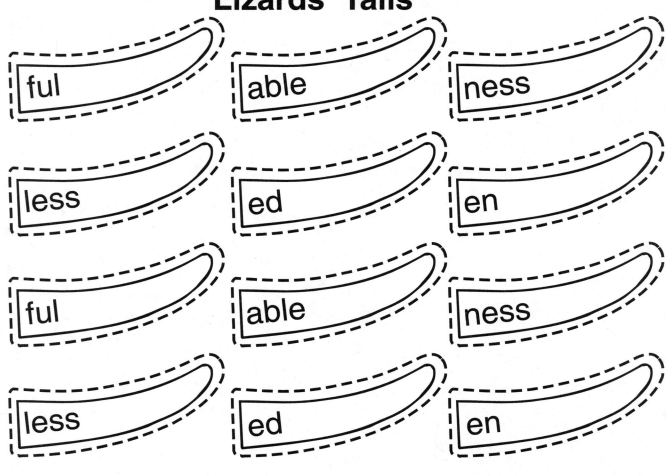

ful	able	ness
less	ed	en
ful	able	ness
less	ed	en

Activity Cards

_____ ful	_____ ful
_____ able	_____ able
_____ ness	_____ ness
_____ ed	_____ ed
_____ en	_____ en
_____ less	_____ less

Cycle Away!

Prefixes

Directions: Two children may play. Take out the clothespins, felt pen or crayon, and the activity cards. Open the folder. Place the clothespins face down. Choose a unicycle to play on. Pick a clothespin in turn and see if its prefix matches a base word on your unicycle. If it does, clip it next to the base word. If it doesn't, put it back. The first one to complete his or her wheel is the winner. Use the felt pen or crayon to write words on an activity card to go with the prefixes. Have your work checked. Wipe off the activity sheet.

A book to read: <u>Bicycle Race</u> by Donald Crews

Cycle Away!

Glue wheel to inside of folder. Leave word edges open for clothespins.

large

tract

pose

pay

please

side

like

scribe

plain

tent

pair

trust

un	re	con	in	sub	pro
ex	dis	de	pre	en	dis

Cut apart and glue to clothespins.

Cycle Away!

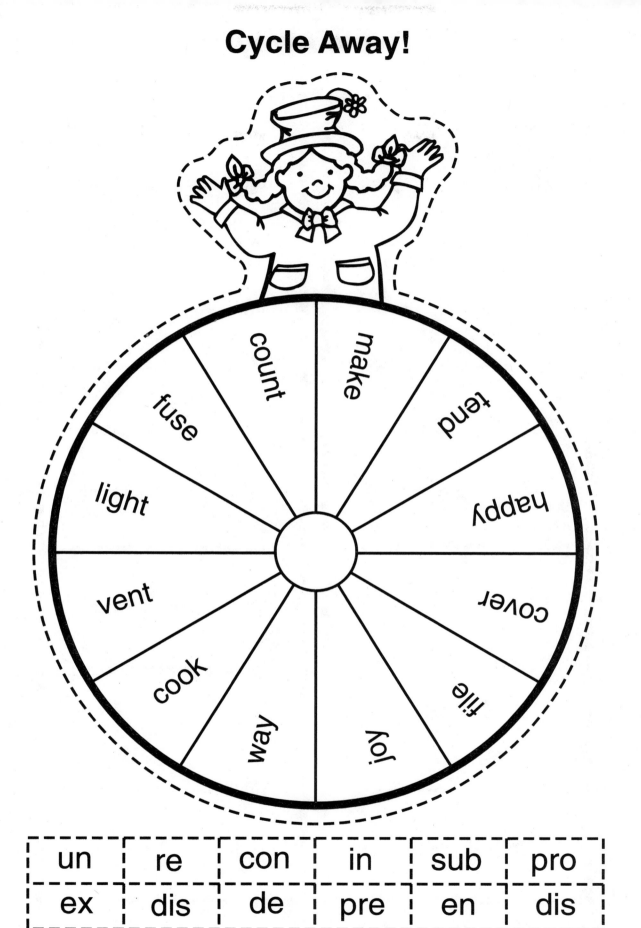

un	re	con	in	sub	pro
ex	dis	de	pre	en	dis

Cycle Away!

Activity Cards

un ———————	un ———————
ex ———————	ex ———————
re ———————	re ———————
dis ———————	dis ———————
con ———————	con ———————
de ———————	de ———————
in ———————	in ———————
pre ———————	pre ———————
sub ———————	sub ———————
en ———————	en ———————
pro ———————	pro ———————
mis ———————	mis ———————

Laminate activity cards.

30

Squirrel at the Wheel

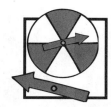

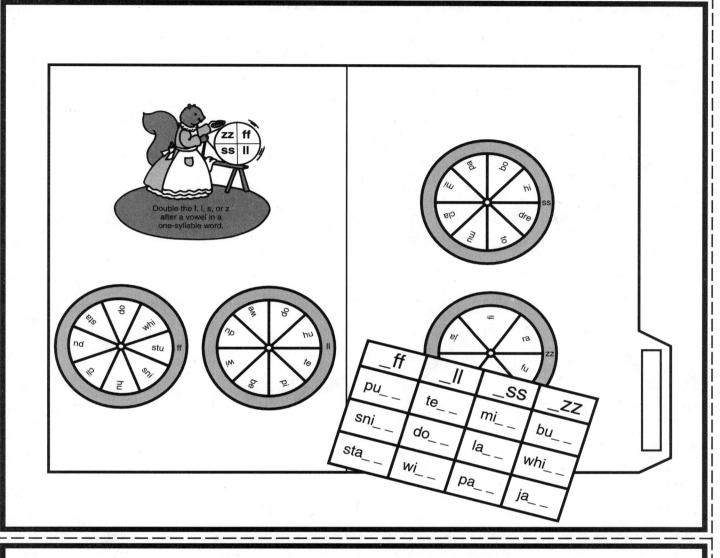

Double the f, l, s, or z after a vowel in a one-syllable word.

_ff	_ll	_ss	_zz
pu_ _	te_ _	mi_ _	bu_ _
sni_ _	do_ _	la_ _	whi_ _
sta_ _	wi_ _	pa_ _	ja_ _

Squirrel at the Wheel

f, l, s, z generalization

Directions: Take out the activity sheet and the felt pen or crayon. Open the folder. Read the direction under the squirrel's spinning wheel. Turn the wheels one at a time and read each word as you make it end with ff, ll, ss, or zz. On the activity sheet, use the felt pen or crayon to add ff, ll, ss, or zz. Wipe off the activity sheet with a soft tissue or rag.

A book to read: <u>The Tale of Squirrel Nutkin</u> by Beatrice Potter

Squirrel at the Wheel

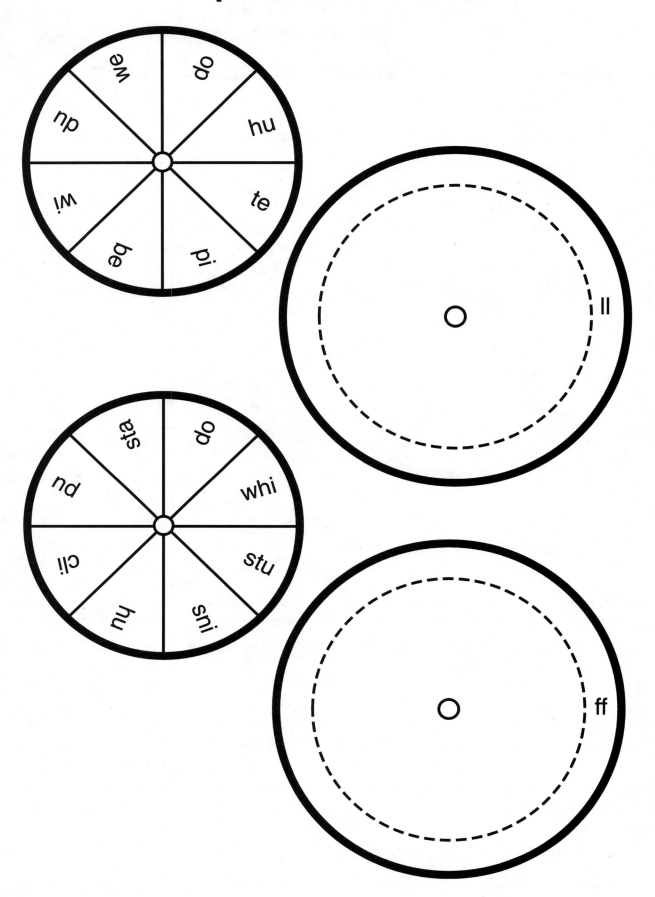

Squirrel at the Wheel

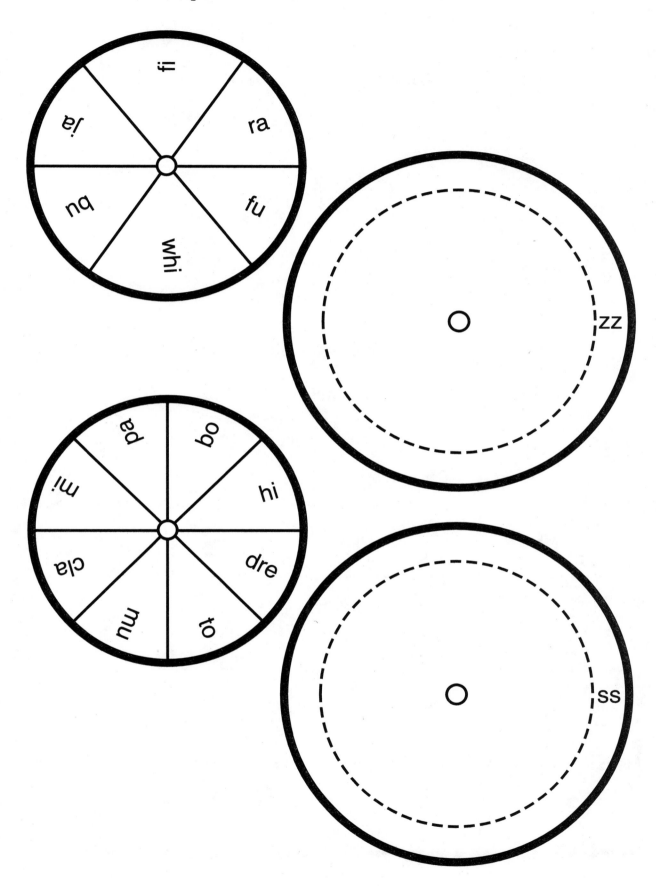

Squirrel at the Wheel

Double the f, l, s, or z
after a vowel in a
one-syllable word.

Activity Card

_ff	_ll	_ss	_zz
pu_ _	te_ _	mi_ _	bu_ _
sni_ _	do_ _	la_ _	whi_ _
sta_ _	wi_ _	pa_ _	ja_ _

31

Use ck, tch, or dge after one short vowel in a one-syllable word.

Goosey Goosey Gander

ck, tch, dge generalization

Directions: Take out the activity card and the felt pen or crayon. Open the folder. Read Goosey Goosey Gander's sign. Turn the ck, tch, and dge wheels. Read each word you make. For the activity card, use the felt pen or crayon to write ck, tch, or dge after the vowel in each word. Wipe off the activity card with a soft tissue or rag.

A book to read: The Day the Goose Got Loose by Reeve Lindbergh

Goosey Goosey Gander

Use ck, tch, or dge
after one short vowel in
a one-syllable word.

tch

ck

dge

wi

clo

sta

de

np

sna

du

li

to

ck

Goosey Goosey Gander

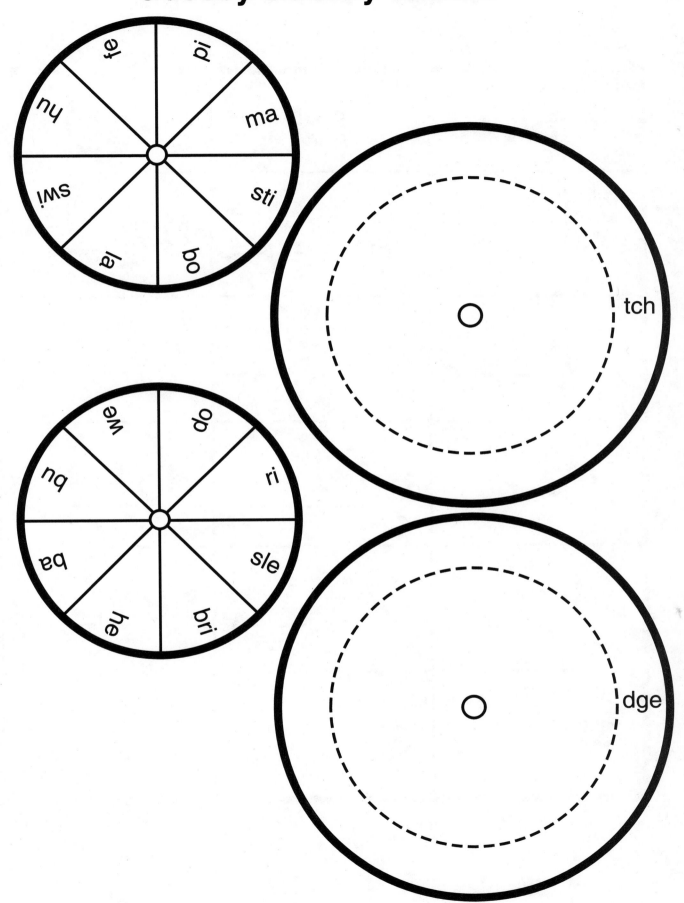

Goosey Goosey Gander

ck	tch	dge
du _ _	pi _ _ _	ba _ _ _
lo _ _	ma _ _ _	fu _ _ _
de _ _	fe _ _ _	do _ _ _
li _ _	bo _ _ _	he _ _ _
sna _ _	sti _ _ _	bri _ _ _

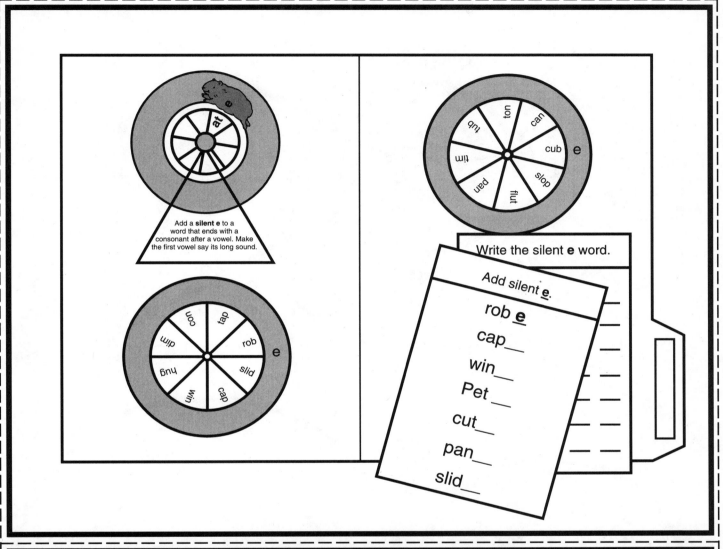

Add a **silent e** to a word that ends with a consonant after a vowel. Make the first vowel say its long sound.

Write the silent **e** word.

Add silent **e**.

rob **e**

cap___

win___

Pet___

cut___

pan___

slid___

Hamster's Wheel

Silent e generalization

Directions: Take out the activity cards and the felt pen or crayon. Open the folder. Read the directions on Hamster's wheel. Turn the wheels and read the silent e words you make. For the activity card with words, use the felt pen or crayon to add a silent e to each word. For the activity card with pictures, write the silent e word. Wipe off the cards with a soft tissue or rag.

A book to read: The Wild Hamster by Alain Vaes

Hamster's Wheel

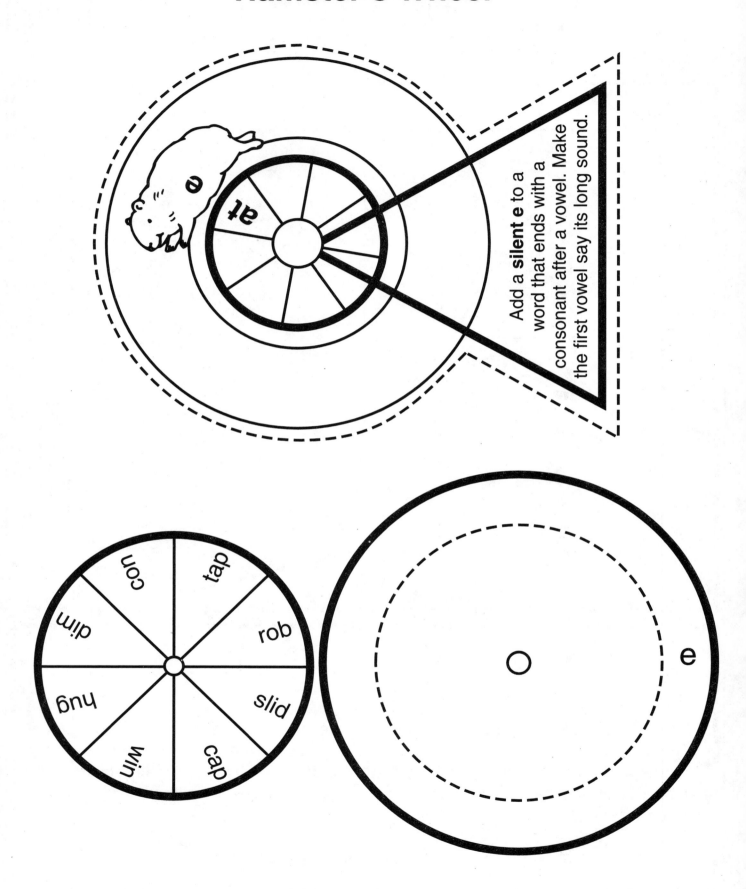

Add a **silent e** to a word that ends with a consonant after a vowel. Make the first vowel say its long sound.

at

e

con
tap
dim
rob
hug
slid
win
cap

e

Hamster's Wheel

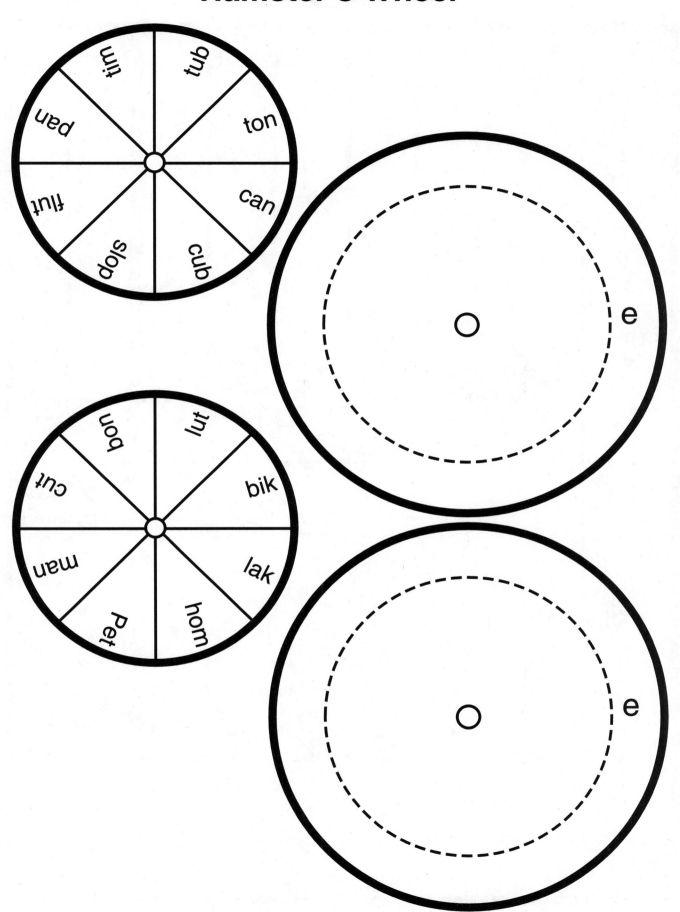

135

Hamster's Wheel

Write the silent e word.

Add silent e.

rob <u>e</u>

cap__

win__

Pet__

cut__

pan__

slid__

Gingerbread Twins

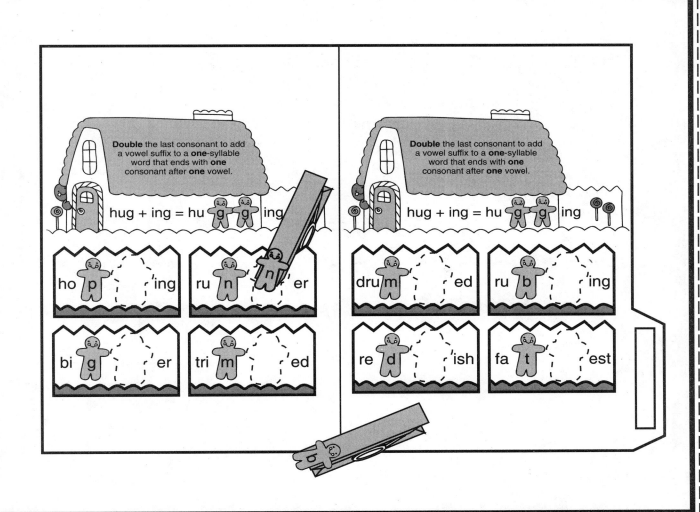

Gingerbread Twins

Doubling the last consonant to add a vowel suffix

Directions: Take out the clothespins. Place them face up. Open the folder. Read the direction on the gingerbread house. For each word, clip on a clothespin that will double the last consonant after the vowel to add a vowel suffix. Check the sample. Read each word you make. Write some of your words on another piece of paper.

A book to read: The Gingerbread Boy by Paul Galdone

Gingerbread Twins

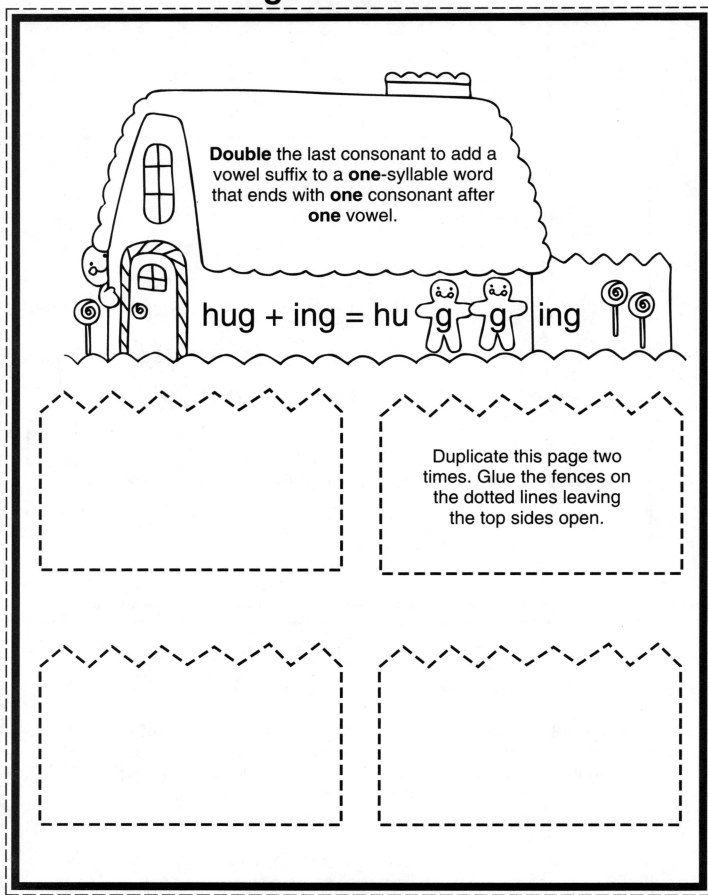

Double the last consonant to add a vowel suffix to a **one**-syllable word that ends with **one** consonant after **one** vowel.

hug + ing = hu g g ing

Duplicate this page two times. Glue the fences on the dotted lines leaving the top sides open.

Gingerbread Twins

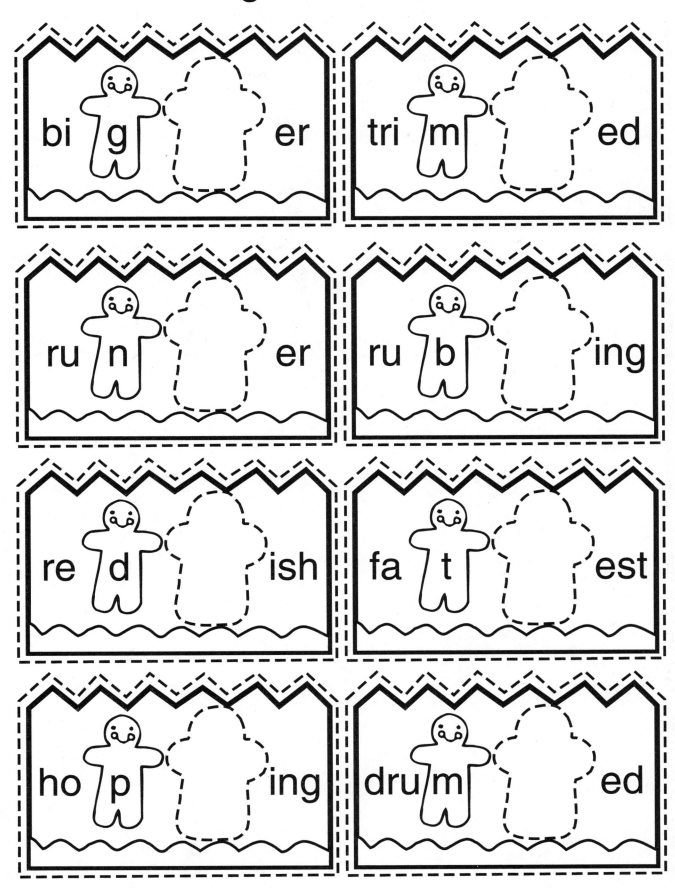

bi g er

tri m ed

ru n er

ru b ing

re d ish

fa t est

ho p ing

dru m ed

Gingerbread Twins

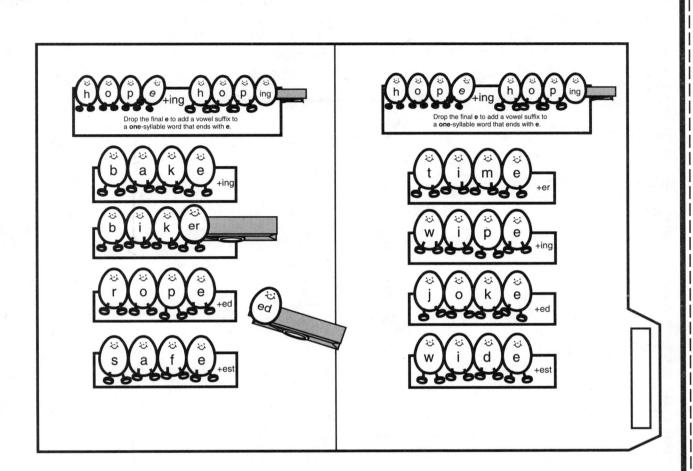

Humpty Dumpty

Final e spelling rule

Directions: Take out the clothespin suffixes. Place them face up. Open the folder. Read the directions on Humpty Dumpty's wall. Clip on each matching suffix, covering the final e. Check the sample. Read the word. Write some of the words on another piece of paper.

A book to read: <u>Humpty Dumpty</u> by Miko Imai

Humpty Dumpty

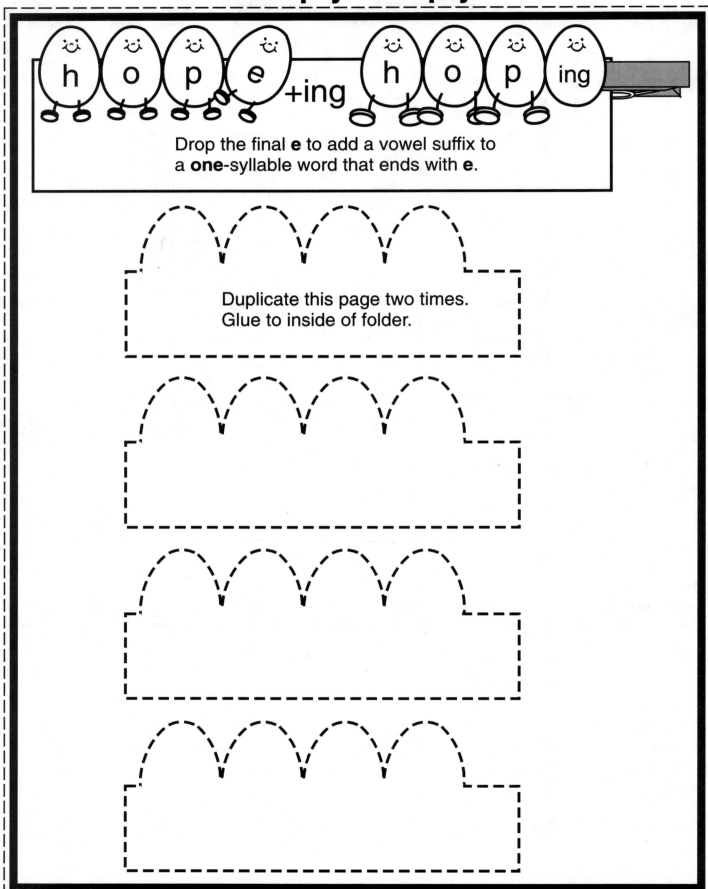

Drop the final **e** to add a vowel suffix to a **one**-syllable word that ends with **e**.

Duplicate this page two times.
Glue to inside of folder.

Humpty Dumpty

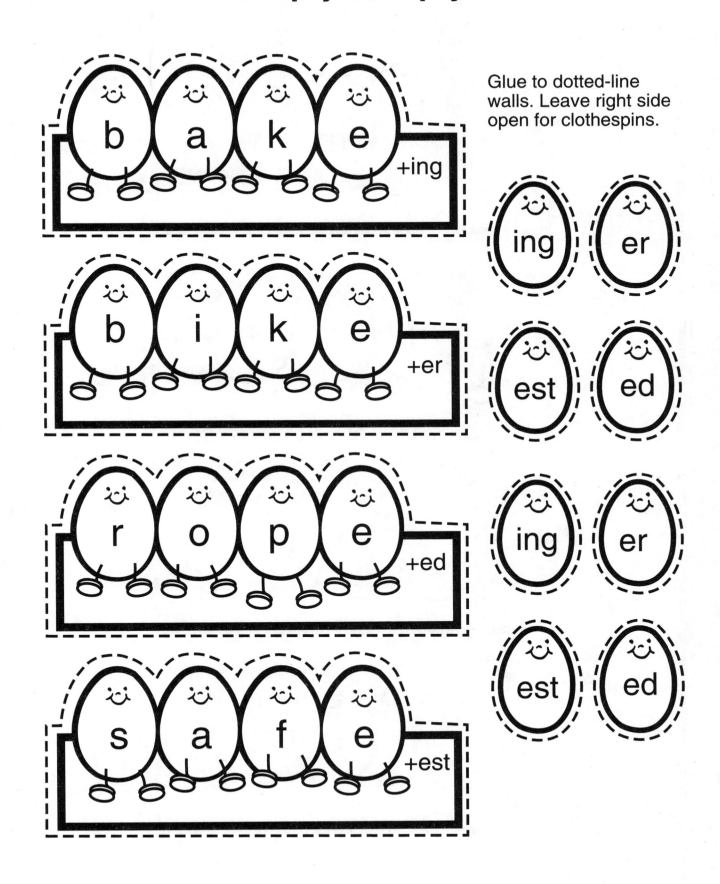

Glue to dotted-line walls. Leave right side open for clothespins.

Humpty Dumpty

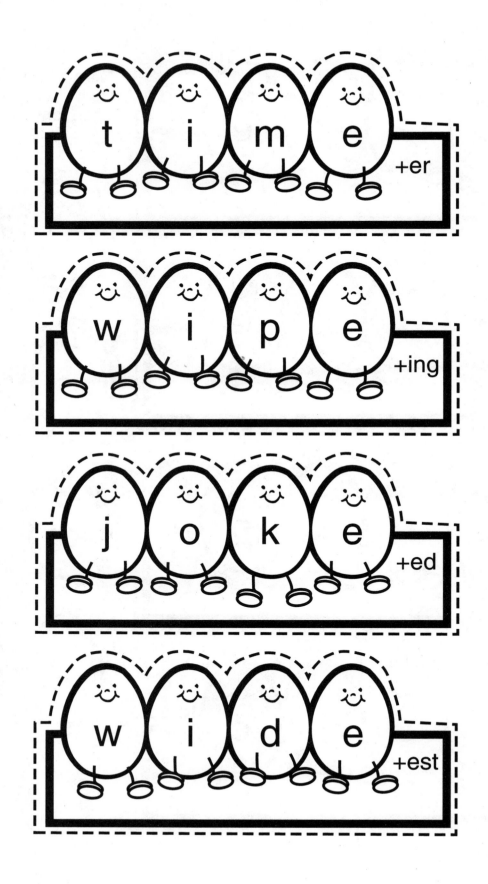